1985

Orienting Students to Co

W9-DFT-352

M. Lee Upcraft, *Editor*

NEW DIRECTIONS FOR STUDENT SERVICES

URSULA DELWORTH and GARY R. HANSON, *Editors-in-Chief*

Number 25, March 1984

Paperback sourcebooks in
The Jossey-Bass Higher Education Series

ᚹ

Jossey-Bass Inc., Publishers
San Francisco • Washington • London

LIBRARY
College of St. Francis
JOLIET, ILL.

M. Lee Upcraft (Ed.).
Orienting Students to College.
New Directions for Student Services, no. 25.
San Francisco: Jossey-Bass, 1984.

New Directions for Student Services Series
Ursula Delworth and Gary R. Hanson, *Editors-in-Chief*

New Directions for Student Services (publication number USPS
449-070) is published quarterly by Jossey-Bass Inc., Publishers.
Second-class postage rates paid at San Francisco, California,
and at additional mailing offices.

Correspondence:
Subscriptions, single-issue orders, change of address notices, undelivered
copies, and other correspondence should be sent to Subscriptions,
Jossey-Bass Inc., Publishers, 433 California Street, San Francisco
California 94104.

Editorial correspondence should be sent to the Editors-in-Chief,
Ursula Delworth, University Counseling Service, Iowa
Memorial Union, University of Iowa, Iowa City, Iowa 52242
or Gary R. Hanson, Office of the Dean of Students,
Student Services Building, Room 101, University of Texas
at Austin, Austin, Texas 78712.

Library of Congress Catalogue Card Number LC 83-82739

International Standard Serial Number ISSN 0164-7970

International Standard Book Number ISBN 87589-786-x

Cover art by Willi Baum

Manufactured in the United States of America

Ordering Information

The paperback sourcebooks listed below are published quarterly and can be ordered either by subscription or single-copy.

Subscriptions cost $35.00 per year for institutions, agencies, and libraries. Individuals can subscribe at the special rate of $25.00 per year *if payment is by personal check.* (Note that the full rate of $35.00 applies if payment is by institutional check, even if the subscription is designated for an individual.) Standing orders are accepted. Subscriptions normally begin with the first of the four sourcebooks in the current publication year of the series. When ordering, please indicate if you prefer your subscription to begin with the first issue of the *coming* year.

Single copies are available at $8.95 when payment accompanies order, and *all single-copy orders under $25.00 must include payment.* (California, New Jersey, New York, and Washington, D.C., residents please include appropriate sales tax.) For billed orders, cost per copy is $8.95 plus postage and handling. (Prices subject to change without notice.)

Bulk orders (ten or more copies) of any individual sourcebook are available at the following discounted prices: 10–49 copies, $8.05 each; 50–100 copies, $7.15 each; over 100 copies, *inquire.* Sales tax and postage and handling charges apply as for single copy orders.

To ensure correct and prompt delivery, all orders must give either the *name of an individual* or an *official purchase order number.* Please submit your order as follows:

Subscriptions: specify series and year subscription is to begin.
Single Copies: specify sourcebook code (such as, SS8) and first two words of title.

Mail orders for United States and Possessions, Latin America, Canada, Japan, Australia, and New Zealand to:
Jossey-Bass Inc., Publishers
433 California Street
San Francisco, California 94104

Mail orders for all other parts of the world to:
Jossey-Bass Limited
28 Banner Street
London EC1Y 8QE

New Directions for Student Services Series
Ursula Delworth and Gary R. Hanson, *Editors-in-Chief*

Contents

Editor's Notes

Most colleges and universities give some attention to the new students they admit. Orientation programs vary in scope, timing, length, and content, but most emphasize academic and social adjustment as well as familiarization with the institution's facilities, programs, and services. Unfortunately, many institutions give very little help to entering students, limiting their programs to a few days before classes begin and focusing on the traditional entering student, just out of high school, away from home for the first time, and from the middle class.

As higher education faces declining enrollments, many institutions are not only stepping up their recruiting efforts but also considering how to keep students once they are enrolled. There is increasing evidence, to be reviewed in this sourcebook, that when entering students participate in orientation programs and activities, they increase their chances of academic success. Thus, institutions must develop comprehensive orientation programs that meet the needs of all students, including not only traditional entering students but minority, disabled, returning adult, and transfer students.

The purpose of this sourcebook is to provide the orientation practitioner with the knowledge and methods to develop comprehensive and effective orientation programs and activities that enhance retention and facilitate personal growth and development. There are countless suggestions for specific programs and activities collected from institutions all over the country.

More important, there is a framework presented within which orientation can be planned and organized to meet the needs of all entering students.

In the first chapter, M. Lee Upcraft, Peter Garland, and Joni Finney summarize the societal context of higher education in the eighties and review the factors that influence students in college as they make the transition from their previous environment to the collegiate environment. They present a model of student development that includes the typical issues and problems of entering students.

In Chapter Two, M. Lee Upcraft and William Farnsworth offer a definition of and rationale for orientation and review the basic goals and components of a comprehensive orientation program. Effective methods for delivering programs and activities are presented as well as effective means of evaluation.

In Chapter Three, Betty Moore, Patricia Peterson, and Robert Wirag review the needs of traditional entering students and offer suggestions for appropriate programs and activities.

Doris Wright discusses the needs and problems of minority students in Chapter Four. She reviews the historical and societal context within which minority students attend college and the ways in which institutions can make orientation programs and activities relevant to minority student needs.

In Chapter Five, Brenda Hameister discusses ways in which orientation for disabled students, with their increased access to higher education, should strike a balance between special programs and activities and participation in mainstream events.

The needs and problems of returning adult students are discussed in Chapter Six by Beverly Greenfeig and Barbara Goldberg, who offer a wide variety of orientation programs and activities for this newer population in higher education.

In Chapter Seven, Charlene Harrison and Kenneth Varcoe review the often forgotten needs of transfer students and suggest ways in which orientation programs and activities should be initiated and adapted to meet their special needs.

In the final chapter, M. Lee Upcraft reviews what has been presented in this sourcebook and offers suggestions and recommendations for future considerations.

Some readers will note the absence of the term *freshmen* in this sourcebook. Although this label is traditionally used to describe someone new to the collegiate environment, we have avoided its use because it smacks of sexism and because it implies the traditional, eighteen-year-old, fresh-out-of-high-school student. Instead, we use the term *entering student*, which we feel better describes all students who are new to the collegiate environment.

Many people contributed to the preparation of this sourcebook. I am especially appreciative of the time and effort expended by the authors. Ursula Delworth, consulting editor of the *New Directions for Student Services* series, was especially helpful to me in developing the proposal for this edition and providing general support and encouragement. Gary Hanson and Ursula Delworth served as excellent editors for the final draft. Jean Hoffman, Stephanie Moyer, Lillian Upcraft, and Kirsten Upcraft's help in typing drafts was greatly appreciated.

M. Lee Upcraft
Editor

M. Lee Upcraft is director of Counseling and Health Services of Pennsylvania State University and a member of the graduate faculty. He has been responsible for the student and parent orientation programs at Penn State since 1971 and has conducted extensive research on entering students.

Orientation planners must understand the societal context
within which students of the 1980s attend college as well
as the influences of the collegiate environment and principles
of student development.

Orientation: A Context

M. Lee Upcraft
Joni E. Finney
Peter Garland

If we are to develop orientation programs and activities that enhance retention and personal development, we must understand the context within which students study and learn in college. This chapter will summarize the societal context of higher education of the 1980s and will review the various factors that influence students in college; their backgrounds and experiences prior to college and the influences on them once they are enrolled. We will present a model of student development describing the typical issues and problems of entering students that can be used as a basis for orienting students to college.

College Students and Society

Perhaps through the media, recent college generations have gained stereotyped images. In the 1950s, the terms *Joe College* and *Betty Coed* stereotyped college students' life-style and outlook. In the 1960s, the stereotype was the political radical with long hair and patched jeans protesting war and the existing social order. In the 1970s, the stereotype pictured the "me" generation of students seeking personal rewards

M. L. Upcraft (Ed.). *Orienting Students to College.* New Directions for
Student Services, no. 25. San Francisco: Jossey-Bass, March 1984.

5

and obsessed with themselves. The stereotype of the 1980s is of a generation seeking a financially secure future in a time of diminishing expectations, which was described by Arthur Levine as "vocomania" (Levine, 1980).

While each of these stereotypes is an overgeneralization, each has an element of truth. Each reflects the greater society in which it existed; each remains a picture of that society. The students of the 1950s reflected a society seeking peace and economic security after a generation of depression and war. The 1960s generation reflected an increasingly affluent and well-educated society in which youth questioned and tried to change its directions and priorities. The 1970s generation mirrored a society that sought to change its focus from the group to the individual. And now, the students of the 1980s reflect a society that may have realized the limits of its growth and that seeks to preserve what it has attained.

In the past twenty years, a number of significant events and changes, many of them economic, have affected our social, political, and moral order. Watergate, Vietnam, diminishing confidence in political leaders, "stagflation," unemployment, recessions, economic uncertainty, and sophisticated technology resulting in increased dependence on computers and information systems are among the many phenomena that have changed and influenced society.

Students of the 1950s, 1960s, and 1970s were reflections of the society in which they existed. They influenced society and society influenced them. Thus, if we are to understand the students of the 1980s and they are to understand themselves, we must analyze the major changes taking place in our society and their effects on students. We have chosen the five changes that have had the greatest implications for higher education.

The Industrial Society Is Changing into an Information Society. It is evident that this country no longer dominates the world's economic order as it once did. Dependence on industrial production is waning, while reliance upon information and its processing is growing. We are witnessing the birth of a new economic order. The conversion of America from an industrial to an information society will be as profound as the earlier change from an agricultural to an industrial society (Naisbitt, 1982).

Students entering college today must recognize this change in the traditional economic order and the implications it has for education and career preparation. Thus, many students must guess which careers will lead to economic security. They must become adept at using and understanding computers and information systems. They must recognize the need for continuing their education as traditional jobs become obsolete or redirected. Adult students may return to college as a direct result of the information age's influence on their careers. Entering students must be aware of the demands that this profound change has on career preparation and future life-styles.

Society Is Now Dealing with the Legacy of the Baby Boom. The 74 million men and women born in the 1946–1964 post-war baby boom represent almost one-third of our nation's population. This boom generation has swelled and strained our institutions as we have attempted to accommodate and absorb it. Students in the traditional college age group are now entering college after the baby boom generation has joined an increasingly competitive work force. Today's students can no longer assume they will find a job; advance within that job; or support a home, family, and life-style equal to or better than that of their parents. Today's students, perhaps for the first time in recent history, may not take for granted these elements of the American dream.

While students may enter colleges and universities with many of the same expectations as their older brothers and sisters, they must realize that things will be difficult for them. The American dream may have to be redefined. The priorities of the society in which they were raised will be different as its members age and attention is directed away from youth to middle age.

Sex Roles Are Changing, Particularly for Women. The traditional roles of male as provider and female as nurturer are being challenged and changed in today's society. More and more women are becoming breadwinners, while more and more men are assuming greater responsibility for their families. Women, even more than men, are being called upon to fulfill a range of roles from provider to nurturer, resulting in role confusion and ambiguity. Women can now exercise freedom of choice over the selection and pursuit of a career, whether or not to marry or have children, and how to participate fully in relationships with men, both in the home and the workplace. In reviewing recent literature on women and careers, Blaska (1978) found that 50 to 70 percent of entering female students desire either a career or both a career and a family. Women are not simply working but are participating fully in their careers as professionals.

Entering students can now select from a broader range of accepted sex roles and expected behaviors. But choice among different and often conflicting roles, particularly for women, may lead to ambiguity, confusion, and stress. Some may choose to do it all, while others may choose to remain within traditional roles. For all, however, changes in role expectations will create a different life-style for both men and women.

Personal Issues Are of More Concern Than Societal Issues. Society is moving from a period of concern about social issues to a primary focus on personal issues. We have been described as being in an age of the "new narcissism" (Lasch, 1978), typified by "meism" (Levine, 1980), while college students are described as the "now" or "me" generation (Suchinsky, 1982). Levine (1980) suggests that the 1980s is a period of "individual ascendancy" emphasizing hedonism and the primacy of duty to the self, as opposed to a period of "community ascendancy" which emphasizes asceticism and the primacy of duty to others. This era of individual ascendancy is characterized by obsessive concern with physical well-being, which is evident in the interest in fitness and dieting. Interpersonal relationships are more transitory, trivial, and violent. Competition for financial security and professional advancement leads to a willingness to sacrifice others for personal gain. At the same time, personal fulfillment becomes more important than the benefit of spouses, children, and friends.

All of this is not lost on today's college students. They are more competitive in the classroom and less willing to help each other. They are struggling to go first class on the Titanic even as they recognize that the ship may be doomed; very few are predisposed to attempt to save it (Levine, 1980). If the computer is the symbol of the information age, perhaps the Walkman is the symbol of today's college students, for it allows them to live in their own world while shutting out the broader world.

The Rapid Rate of Social Change Is Overwhelming. Change is inevitable. However, changes occur so rapidly that there is little time to understand and react to them before things have changed again. The rate of change is accelerating. The future belongs to those who plan for, understand, and quickly adapt to change.

The implications for today's students are enormous. They must not only go to college to get specialized training but they must get enough general education to adapt to changing conditions. They must think in terms of several jobs and two or three careers and must prepare for reeducation and retraining. Planning for the future will be increasingly difficult and will create confusion that may lead to indecision about career choice and uncertainty about the value of an education. Thus, we must understand the rapid changes occurring in society in order to help students adapt to changes in their lives and careers.

To be sure, the influence of college itself is very powerful, but so is the society in which today's entering students were raised. Thus, societal realities must be incorporated into thinking about and planning orientation programs and activities for entering students.

The Influence of College

A college influences entering students in two fundamental ways: through the kinds of students it admits and through the influence it exerts once they are enrolled. Put another way, what happens to entering students is some combination of who they are before they come to college and what happens to them after they arrive. In this sense, the admissions officer may exert as much influence as faculty, administrative staff, and fellow students.

To understand how students succeed in college, it is necessary to understand the influence of their backgrounds and experiences prior to college. Newcomb (1966) argued that these variables are the most influential determiners of what happens to students after they arrive in college. They include race, prior academic achievement, motivation, parents' education and income, and sex (Trent and Medsker, 1968; Feldman and Newcomb, 1969; Astin, 1972). In general, white, high-achieving, highly motivated, male students from affluent and educated families are more likely to succeed than other students.

Family influence is especially important. Students who maintain compatible relationships with their families are more likely to succeed in college than those who do not (Upcraft, Peterson, and Moore, 1981b). Families can be helpful by providing emotional support and by helping with major and career decisions and with personal problems. Traditional entering students may develop tensions with their parents over career choice, academic performance, money, sexuality, or values, not to mention the increasing number of students affected by divorced or separated parents. Returning adult students may develop tensions with their spouses over new economic realities, redefinitions of spouse and parent roles, and childcare and the problems of being a single parent. Students with no family ties at all may have problems coping without the support of a family.

To provide effective help to entering students, it is important to consider where they come from and what they bring with them. If an institution attracts students whose prior backgrounds and characteristics predict high success in college, programs and activities may move in a different direction than if the institution attracts students whose backgrounds predict a lower success. Too often, too little attention is paid to entering students' backgrounds and characteristics, assuming too much homogeneity. As a result, orientation programs and activities often miss the mark.

Once students enroll, we often misunderstand, underestimate, or ignore how institutional characteristics influence entering students. In general, large, less selective, public, coeducational, commuting universities have a negative impact on such things as persistence, personal contacts with faculty, quality of instruction, and opportunities to work with faculty (Astin, 1968, 1972). The goals and purposes of an institution can also have an impact. When a college has a distinctive character and explicit goals, it can more successfully shape and change student behavior (Hochbaum, 1968). Thus, institutions whose demographics mitigate against student success have an even greater obligation to develop orientation programs and activities that help students succeed.

An institution's climate, as well as its characteristics, exerts a very powerful influence on entering students. Although global measures of campus climate may be generally helpful (Pace and Stern, 1958; Astin, 1968; Clark and Trow, 1966), it is probably more useful to identify specific elements of institutional climate that enhance student success. In general, student success is enhanced by a campus climate that (1) promotes student-to-student interaction (Feldman and Newcomb, 1969); (2) promotes faculty-student contact (Pascarella and Terenzini, 1977; Terenzini and Pascarella, 1979); (3) offers on-campus, residential living (Chickering, 1974; Astin, 1977; Upcraft, Peterson, and Moore, 1981b); and (4) offers extensive extracurricular opportunities (Winter, McClelland, and Stewart, 1981; Lenning, Sauer, and Beal, 1980; Ramist, 1980).

Entering students are also encountering an environment that is physically and interpersonally different from anything they have ever experienced before, an environment that is more homogeneous and more intense. Some students will be more susceptible to this environment than others who will seem almost immune. Entering students will affect and change the environment as well. Generally speaking, when there is a congruence between an individual and the campus environment, that student will be happier, better adjusted, and more likely to achieve personal and educational goals (Western Interstate Commission for Higher Education, 1973).

What determines whether or not entering students adapt to their new environment? There are several factors, but undoubtedly the most important is the influence of students on one another. The scope of this influence is enormous. Peer groups help achieve independence from home and family, support or impede academic goals, provide emotional support, develop interpersonal skills, change or reinforce values, and influence career decisions (Feldman and Newcomb, 1969).

Peer groups exercise this influence by establishing norms and providing behavior guidelines that are reinforced through direct rewards—

emotional support, acceptance, and inclusion, for example—and punishment—rejection, scapegoating, and exclusion, for example. In effect, entering students transfer some control over themselves to the peer group and become subject to its influence. That influence has a pervasive effect on students' success in college.

Too often it is assumed that peer groups influence only late adolescent, entering students, fresh out of high school and away from home for the first time. On the contrary, returning adult students and transfers often suffer because of their isolation from each other. They have difficulty finding other students with whom they share common interests and concerns. They don't feel comfortable with late-adolescent students, yet need support from peers with similar backgrounds, interests, problems, and circumstances. Many institutions help these students find each other because they know the importance of peer group influence.

Other factors aid in helping the student cope with the new collegiate environment. Living in residence halls, in general, is a positive influence. Upcraft and Pilato (1982) summarized the evidence and concluded that entering students living in residence halls, when compared to those living elsewhere, (1) are more satisfied with their living environment and their college experience; (2) earn higher grades and are less likely to drop out, even when differences in prior achievement and academic abilities are taken into account; (3) have more contact with faculty; (4) have fewer emotional problems; (5) have more contact with other students and a more satisfied social life; (6) have higher educational aspirations; and (7) participate more in student and recreational activities.

Other factors that contribute to the academic and personal success of entering students include establishing close friends (Billson and Terry, 1982; Fiedler and Vance, 1981), especially during the first month of enrollment (Simpson, Baker, and Mellinger, 1980). There is also evidence, which will be reviewed in Chapter Two, that participation in orientation enhances academic achievement, retention, and personal development. Additional critical factors include belonging to student organizations (Billson and Terry, 1982; Lenning, Sauer, and Beal, 1980), involvement in social activities (Jeanotte, 1982; Terenzini, Pascarella, and Lorang, 1982), involvement in cultural activities (Winter, McClelland, and Stewart, 1981), attending lectures (Hyatt, 1980), using facilities (Churchill and Iwai, 1981), and general participation in extracurricular and campus activities (Winter, McClelland, and Stewart, 1981; Lenning, Sauer, and Beal, 1980; Ramist, 1981; University of California, 1980).

In summary, if institutions are committed to helping entering students make a successful transition to the collegiate environment, they must consider the characteristics and backgrounds of the students they admit; institutional characteristics; and the campus climate, including the influence of the peer group, the living setting, and involvement in campus activities.

Developmental Dimensions

Successful orientation programs and activities must also be based on a thorough knowledge and understanding of entering students' personal and academic development. Orientation planners must go beyond their own undergraduate and professional experiences in establishing a conceptual basis for their orientation programs and activities. They should read and understand such theorists as Erikson, Chickering, Perry, Kohlberg, Loevinger, Douglas Heath, Roy Heath, Madison, and Brawer. The reader is encouraged to read original sources or extended summaries such as those by Knefelkamp, Widick, Parker (1978), and Upcraft and Pilato (1982).

However, there are some problems in translating student development theory into orientation programs. First, no one theory is inclusive enough to be applied to the exclusion of the others. Second, even with an eclectic theory, students may have trouble relating their experiences to the underlying psychodynamics of their development. Third, some theories have been criticized for generalizing male development inappropriately to female development (Gilligan, 1977), while other theories can't be applied to minority student development (Wright, Chapter Four).

It may be more useful for the orientation practitioner to work from students' own experiences toward student development concepts rather than the other way around. Coons (1971) made this point when he developed his "frame of reference" for working with college students instead of using a universal student development theory. He found that his frame of reference, which was based on how students experience their own development, seemed to "make sense to students themselves" (Coons, 1971, p. 19). A model, rather than a theory, if based on entering students' experiences, can apply to all students, not just late adolescent, mainstream students. When orientation programs are based on student needs and experiences, rather than theories about student development, they are more successful.

The model of student development that the authors have found workable has its roots in several student development theories. Recently, we asked a group of seniors what had been the most important thing they learned from attending college. The most frequent answer was, "I grew up." When asked to be more specific, they replied, "I learned to get along with people" and "I learned more about myself" (Upcraft, Peterson, and Moore, 1981a). These responses from seniors form a good conceptual basis for orienting entering students. Entering students mature in college by developing greater autonomy and establishing a clearer sense of identity.

Entering students, regardless of their backgrounds and prior experiences, are seeking to become more autonomous. Chickering (1972) defines autonomy as the need to be self-sufficient and to establish interdependent relations with others. Traditional entering students may establish their autonomy by achieving independence from parents and peers. Returning adult students may establish their autonomy by preparing for careers that allow them greater freedom and more interdependent relationships with their families. Minority students may establish greater autonomy by becoming less dependent upon the economic oppression of society. Disabled students, through education, may become economically and emotionally independent.

Entering students are also seeking a clearer sense of identity. They are developing a better sense of who they are, or to use Erikson's (1963) term, a sense of ego identity. Erikson argued that a sense of identity is fully developed when the inner sense of self is consistent with its meaning for others. He was referring to the development of youth, but the concept applies to entering students as well. For example, the divorced woman who returns to college may, for the first time, define herself as a career woman as well as a provider and mother. The black student who attends college may, for the first time, see himself as an engineer rather than an unskilled laborer.

Entering students talk about their college experiences as a series of events rather than processes, such as autonomy and identity. They recall specific issues, concerns, fears, and successes rather than inferred psychological dynamics. The traditional entering student says, "I was homesick during the first few weeks." The returning adult student says, "I was afraid I could not compete with all those kids just out of high school." The minority student says, "Going to an all-white college put me up tight." The disabled student says, "Just getting from my dorm to my classes seemed almost impossible at first." They do not say, "My sense of self was so insecure that I was unable to develop interdependent relationships," nor would they attend a program advertised as a way to compensate. They will attend orientation programs that are consistent with what they are thinking and feeling at the time they enroll.

We have identified six major developmental issues, similar although not identical to those developed by Coons, that students must deal with during the college years: (1) developing intellectual and academic competence, (2) establishing and maintaining interpersonal relationships, (3) developing a sex-role identity and sexuality, (4) deciding on a career and life-style, (5) formulating an integrated philosophy of life, and (6) maintaining personal health and wellness. These issues may overlap — deciding what sexual behavior is right or wrong, for example; and not all students deal with these issues all the time. If orientation programs are to be developmentally based, it is necessary to examine each of these issues in more detail.

Developing Academic and Intellectual Competence. Ask entering students what they fear most about going to college and they will probably say, "flunking out." Most students come to college with the sole purpose of preparing for a career by getting good grades and graduating. Many soon recognize that an education is something more than acquiring knowledge and that success in college consists of more than getting good grades. Students learn how to learn and how to synthesize, integrate, criticize, and analyze what they learn. They consider the moral, ethical, and spiritual implications of what they learn. They develop an appreciation for the esthetic side of life. (Chickering, 1972; Lenning and others, 1974; Krathwohl, Bloom, and Masia, 1964; Bowen, 1977; Baird and Hartnett, 1980; Heist and Yonge, 1962; Warren, 1978; Morrill, 1980).

Entering students have some sense of their past academic successes and failures. Many have done well enough to get admitted to college, while others may have been admitted under special admissions criteria. Some may have been away from formal academic settings for some period of time, while others may be fresh from an unsatisfactory experience at another institution. They enter college with varying degrees of confidence and ability. For most, the transition to the college classroom requires an adjustment of their academic routines.

Some students will have more problems in adjusting to the college classroom than others. Classes may be larger, instructors may have different teaching styles, the pace may be faster, written work more frequent, reading assignments more lengthy, standards higher, and competition keener. The responsibility for what is learned may shift from the professor to the student. No one may care whether or not students learn. Entering students may find they lack the necessary skills, motivation, ability, interest, or time to cope with this new academic environment.

Nonacademic demands may also interfere. Traditional entering students, with their new freedom from parental restrictions, may let their social lives overwhelm their academic efforts. Disabled students may expend so much time and energy attending to their personal needs and overcoming their handicaps that little time and energy are left for studying. Minority students may spend so much time and energy battling racial barriers or coping with a majority environment that preparing for class becomes very difficult. Returning adult students may find that being a parent, spouse, and part-time worker may interfere with academic work. Adjustments in daily schedules and priorities may be necessary if students are to succeed in the classroom.

Entering students can become so obsessed with classroom success that they ignore other opportunities for rounding out their education. Their backgrounds and prior experiences may limit their perception of what an education can be, causing them to miss the opportunity to learn how to learn, to consider the moral and ethical implications of what they learn, or to develop esthetic appreciation. These students fail to develop themselves intellectually as well as academically, in spite of the many opportunities to do so.

Orientation programs must help students adjust to the demands of the classroom and teach them how to earn good grades by exposing them to the new academic climate and teaching them how to handle the other aspects of their lives that affect academic success. Orientation programs should encourage students to develop intellectually and to take advantage of the opportunities to become broadly educated people.

Establishing and Maintaining Interpersonal Relationships. Another frequently mentioned worry of entering students is finding new friends. There is evidence that establishing effective interpersonal relationships is an important element in college success (Billson and Terry, 1982; Fiedler and Vance, 1981; Simpson, Baker, and Mellinger, 1980). All entering students, regardless of their backgrounds and experiences, must develop an interpersonal support system with their fellow students and must learn how to relate to faculty and other people in the collegiate environment. There may be roommates to be dealt with and extracurricular activities that require interpersonal skills and cooperation. Perhaps for the first time, entering students must relate to people of different cultural backgrounds, sexual preferences, life experiences, physical disabilities, or skin colors.

Entering students come to college with varying degrees of skill and experience in dealing with people. Traditional entering students, away from home for the first time, are completely uprooted from family and friends thrust into a world of strangers. Even those who stay at home may find conflicts between their two interpersonal worlds. A mother and wife returning to college must develop new friends in similar circumstances while maintaining meaningful yet changing relationships with her husband and children. Minority students must learn to relate to majority students — and in some instances, deal with prejudice — while seeking out other minority students for friendship and support. Disabled students may be rejected because abled students don't feel comfortable around them. Transfer students may feel isolated because they can't find one another and don't find anything in common with traditional entering students.

Entering students must, therefore, become skilled in dealing with others. They must learn how to listen as well as to express themselves. They must learn how to share more intimate thoughts and feelings and to initiate new friendships. They must learn to be assertive without being aggressive. They must be able to develop a capacity for intimacy and be aware of their impact on others. They must develop honesty and integrity in relationships and learn how to end them as well as initiate them. In short, they must develop the interpersonal skills necessary to succeed in college.

Orientation programs must help students establish and maintain interpersonal relationships. They must help entering students find one another and teach them how to relate to people different from themselves. Orientation programs must also help entering students deal with faculty, administrative staff, and other people in the collegiate environment. Orientation planners must recognize that not all entering students are eighteen years old, away from home for the first time, fresh out of high school, and from the middle class. They should create programs that allow all entering students, regardless of their backgrounds and circumstances, to establish and maintain interpersonal relationships.

Developing a Sex-Role Identity and Sexuality. As described earlier, a sense of identity is fully developed when the inner self is consistent with its meaning for others (Erikson, 1963). An important part of a general sense of identity is sexual identity. In addition to the question "Who am I?" entering students often struggle with the masculine and feminine dimensions of their identities. Entering students come from backgrounds that have taught a variety of sexual identities, from traditional to liberated. Because traditional sex roles are being challenged and new ones are still unclear, many entering students become confused and uncertain about their roles as men and women in society.

Traditionally, masculinity and femininity have been considered mutually exclusive personality characteristics, whereas recent evidence (Deutsche and Gilbert, 1976; Bem, 1975) suggests they might be more appropriately considered interdependent characteristics of personality, frequently labeled *androgyny*. Identity can be seen as both instrumental and expressive, assertive and yielding, and both masculine and feminine, as determined by an individual's situation rather than by sex. Research suggests that androgynous college students are more likely than highly sex-typed students to be both high in achievement and affiliation, combining needs for instrumental accomplishments and close personal relationships. An androgynous identity is also associated with lower anxiety, greater self-actualization, and a more positive self-concept than a sex-typed identity (Pettus, 1976).

What does all this mean for the entering student? Although there are clear advantages for an androgynous self-concept, entering students have been raised in a society that has reinforced traditional masculinity as more healthy and productive. There is some evidence that college men are more likely than college women to be described as healthy adults, because society's definition of health is closer to traditional masculinity than traditional femininity. Is it any wonder, then, that women, perhaps more than men, are open to new roles and behaviors once thought inappropriate (Brooks-Gunn and Fisch, 1980)? But it is also unlikely that men can escape the college experience without reconsidering appropriate masculine roles and behaviors.

Entering students come to college with a wide variety of sexual identities, values, and backgrounds. Many have been raised with traditional sex-role identities, while others have been taught more fluid and egalitarian sex roles. There may even be some who have androgynous identities. Many students may be trapped between intellectual androgyny and emotionally sex-restricted identities. For example, some men may accept yielding behavior as appropriate but be unable to yield in practice. Women may accept combining motherhood and a career as appropriate but feel guilty about leaving their children with baby-sitters while they work.

Whatever their backgrounds, entering students are likely to face a stiff challenge to their beliefs about masculinity, femininity, and androgyny. They are presented with new role models, new ideas, and new behaviors, all of which may result in periods of confusion or outright identity crises. There may be prolonged periods when students question career decisions, friendships, family relations, sexual relations and behavior, and self-concepts.

Traditional entering students may have to reevaluate their sexual relationships and sexual behavior. These students must not only learn how to develop healthy and positive sexual relationships but how to avoid the negative consequences of sexual activity, such as unwanted pregnancies and sexually transmitted diseases. Returning adult students may be breaking out of traditional sex roles simply by returning to college. Disabled students may struggle with how their disability affects their identities and their sexual activity. Minority students may find that androgynous and traditional sex roles conflict with minority family and community definitions of masculine and feminine roles.

Orientation programs must help entering students deal with their identities and sex roles. They must provide information about healthy sexual relationships and the possible negative consequences of sexual activity. Orientation programs must also provide an opportunity for entering students to reconsider their identities and sex roles, the societal forces that influence them, and the choices they have. Orientation programs must provide the resources, the context, and the ideas needed to help entering students develop an appropriate sex-role identity.

Deciding on a Career and Life-Style. Although some students enter college admitting they don't know what they want to do, most have some career goal in mind. Even those with a career choice may have had little basis for choosing it. Some students may have been pushed into careers by their families, while others may have picked one just to relieve their anxiety about not having a career choice. Still others may have picked popular or lucrative careers, knowing nothing of what they're really like or what it takes to prepare for them. Returning adult students may be shifting from a known career to an unknown one or planning to return to the work force after a prolonged absence. Disabled students may not know what implications, if any, their disability has for their career choice. Minority students, because of past barriers to education and careers, may not have a clear notion of their chosen careers or what it takes to prepare for them.

College is almost an immediate test of students' career commitment. The fact that a large percentage of students change their majors at least once is some indication of career choice instability. Some students will stay with their original choice and prepare for their chosen field with little difficulty. Others will change because release from family pressure allows them to pursue their real interests, based on their real abilities. Career change may also result from information and experiences gained from courses and faculty contact. Lack of academic success is the major contributor to career choice instability and forces students to change to another field, transfer to another institution, or drop out altogether.

Career choice also has implications for students' life-styles after college, although many students fail to see this connection. They may only see the excitement or financial gain and not the long hours, intense stress, or job insecurity. Returning adults may have entered college precisely because they wanted to discard their current life-style for an improved one. Minority students may choose a career they know will take them from impoverished environments to more attractive ones. Disabled students may choose careers that will lead to more independent lives. Career choice involves not only looking at the career and individual abilities to prepare for it, but the effects of that career on leisure time, special interests, family commitments, and other nonwork aspects of life.

Another issue that has emerged as a student priority of the 1980s is the economic reality of career choice. Choosing a career based on students' interests and abilities is ideal, but more and more students are choosing careers for financial reasons. This may be especially true for returning adults and minority students, whose economic motivation for college may be especially strong, but it is also true for traditional entering students. Horror stories about unemployed college graduates discourage students from selecting careers based solely on interests and abilities. There is some risk, however, in using economic factors alone to choose a career. Setting aside for the moment the unhappiness that may result from choosing a career solely on an economic basis, it is also difficult to predict which careers will be the most lucrative at the time of graduation.

Orientation programs must help students deal with career choice instability and make them aware of the services and programs available to help them select an appropriate career. Although some students will have little difficulty, most will reconsider their choice, hopefully in the light of economic realities and life-style implications. It is the responsibility of orientation programs to help students decide on a career and life-style and to assure them that uncertainty and instability are to be expected.

Maintaining Personal Health and Wellness. Students must be aware of the impact of their life experiences on their physical and emotional well-being; in other words, on their state of wellness. Wellness is defined as (1) being free from symptoms of disease and pain as much as possible, (2) being able to be active—able to do what one wants and what one must at the appropriate time, and (3) being in good spirits most of the time. Wellness is an ongoing process in which one develops and encourages every aspect of body, mind, and feelings to interrelate harmoniously as much of the time as possible (Edlin and Golanty, 1982).

The college experience, for most students, is a stressful one that affects physical and emotional well-being. However, as Selye (1975) points out, not all stress is negative. He differentiates between distress—the negative effects of stress—and eustress—the positive effects of stress. Eustress can be a positive motivating force in entering students' lives, encouraging them to satisfy their needs. However, distress—too much stress—can lead to such problems and diseases as alcohol and drug abuse, chronic headaches, smoking, nutritional disorders, sexual disorders, psychosomatic illnesses, depression, high anxiety, and even suicide. Stress, then, is a double-edged sword that is essential to life and survival, but that is also potentially destructive (Selye, 1975).

By attending college, entering students add additional stresses to their lives. They must enroll in courses, study for exams, worry about grades, and deal with academic failure. They must find new friends; cope with a new environment; get along with their instructors; and deal with career choice, sexuality, and other developmental issues. As a result, personal health and wellness issues are accelerated. Traditional entering students may, for the first time, have complete control over their nutritional habits, alcohol use, and sexual activity, which may lead to weight problems, alcohol abuse, and sexually transmitted diseases. Returning adult students' personal health and wellness may be affected by adding college life to already busy and demanding lives. Minority students may suffer as a result of the added stress of being alone in a majority environment. Disabled students may have to deal with the additional stress of coping with their disability in a new environment. Some students may have prior chronic health or emotional problems that affect college life.

Too often, students think of personal health issues as a series of hazards to be avoided. Few students think of maintaining health and wellness as an active rather than a reactive process. They seldom realize that there is much they can do in their daily routines to maintain health and prevent disease. Being attuned to personal health and wellness is a key to survival in college. Relieving stress through physical activity, such as jogging or playing tennis, may be as important to academic success as studying hard. Developing moderate and responsible drinking or eating behaviors may be just as important as taking good notes in class. Unfortunately, many students don't think about habits of wellness until a problem develops and the solution is much more difficult.

Orientation programs must help entering students understand that maintaining personal health and wellness is an active process, involving disease and injury prevention and health promotion practices, which enables them to lead enriched lives during and after college. They should be made aware of the additional stress that being a college student brings and the importance of dealing with that stress if they are to succeed in college. Students should be informed of campus services and programs that promote wellness and that help them with physical and emotional problems.

Formulating an Integrated Philosophy of Life. Chickering (1972) sees college as a time when students develop a clearer sense of purpose and clarify personally valid sets of beliefs that have internal consistency and provide a guide for behavior. Both Perry (1970) and Kohlberg (1971) have described the stages of the ethical and moral development of college students. Entering students must reconsider what is right and wrong, their priorities in life, their religious and spiritual beliefs, and how they fit into the larger order of things in the universe. However, developing an integrated philosophy of life is not usually very high on the list of entering students' concerns, if it can be found on the list at all. Yet few students will escape college without dealing with some of these issues.

Traditional entering students may, for the first time, be free to choose values and behaviors without parental influence. They may astonish their parents with new values, beliefs, and behaviors, while others will simply maintain what they were taught at home. Returning adult students may reconsider their values and beliefs and unsettle their spouses and children with redefinitions of themselves. Minority students may become more aware of how society has mistreated them, how that has affected what they believe, and how they think of themselves. Disabled students may reconsider how their disability affects what they believe and how they live. Transfer students' attitudes and values may change as they move from one institution to another.

Some entering students will respond to these challenges by rethinking and reformulating their values and beliefs. There may be periods of experimentation, confusion, and disruption, with great stress placed on families and peers. Other students will respond in a more gradual way, while still others will not respond at all. Regardless of their response to these challenges, students should leave college with values, beliefs, and self-concepts that are internalized and integrated. These values, beliefs, and self-concepts will be owned by the student and will have internal consistency. There will also be consistency between what students believe and how they behave.

Of all the developmental dimensions described in this chapter, formulating an integrated philosophy of life is probably the most difficult to incorporate into an orientation program. It is a lifelong process and is not easily approached with entering students who have other things on their minds. Nevertheless, orientation programs must at least introduce the issue, stimulating entering students to think more about what they believe and how those beliefs will be challenged while they are in college.

Summary

In this chapter, we have discussed the societal context of higher education in the 1980s and reviewed how students' backgrounds and characteristics affect their college development. We have also reviewed how the characteristics and climate of a college influence entering students and the typical developmental issues they must deal with while enrolled. All of this information is essential to developing effective orientation programs that enhance academic and personal success in college. Without such a framework, orientation becomes a potpourri of unrelated and ineffective activities that will have little influence on the lives of entering students.

References

Astin, A. W. *The College Environment.* Washington, D.C.: American Council on Education, 1968.

Astin, A. W. "The Measured Effects of Higher Education." *The Annals of the American Academy of Political and Social Science,* 1972, *404,* 1–20.

Astin, A. W. *Four Critical Years: Effects of College Beliefs, Attitudes, and Knowledge.* San Francisco: Jossey-Bass, 1977.

Baird, L. L., and Hartnett, R. T. *Understanding Student and Faculty Life.* San Francisco: Jossey-Bass, 1980.

Bem, S. L. "Sex Role Adaptability: One Consequence of Psychological Androgyny." *Journal of Personality and Social Psychology,* 1975, 634–643.

Billson, J. M., and Terry, M. B. "In Search of the Silken Purse: Factors in Attrition Among First Generation Students." *College and University,* 1982, *58* (Fall), 57–75.

Blaska, B. "College Women's Career and Marriage Aspirations: A Review of the Literature." *Journal of College Student Personnel,* 1978, *19* (4), 302–305.

Bowen, H. R. *Investment in Learning.* San Francisco: Jossey-Bass, 1977.

Brooks-Gunn, V., and Fisch, M. "Psychological Androgyny and College Students — Judgments of Mental Health." *Sex Roles,* 1980, *6* (4), 575–580.

Chickering, A. *Education and Identity.* San Francisco: Jossey-Bass, 1972.

Chickering, A. *Commuting Versus Residential Students.* San Francisco: Jossey-Bass, 1974.

Churchill, W. D., and Iwai, S. I. "College Attrition, Student Use of Campus Facilities, and a Consideration of Self-Reported Personal Problems." *Research in Higher Education,* 1981, *14* (4), 353–365.

Clark, B. R., and Trow, M. "The Organizational Context." In T. M. Newcomb and E. K. Wilson (Eds.), *College Peer Groups: Problems and Prospects for Research.* Chicago: Aldine, 1966.

Coons, F. "The Development Tasks of the College Student." In D. DeCoster and P. Mable (Eds.), *Student Development and Education in Residence Halls.* Washington, D.C.: American College Personnel Association, 1971

Deutsche, C. J., and Gilbert, L. A. "Sex-Role Stereotypes: Effect on Perceptions of Self and Others and on Personal Adjustment." *Journal of Counseling Psychology,* 1976, *23.*

Edlin, G. P., and Golanty, E. *Health and Wellness: A Holistic Appraoch.* Boston: Science Books International, 1982.

Erikson, E. *Childhood and Society.* New York: Norton, 1963.

Feldman, K. A., and Newcomb, T. M. (Eds.). *The Impact of College on Students.* San Francisco: Jossey-Bass, 1969.

Fiedler, D., and Vance, E. B. "To Stay or Leave the University: Every Student's Dilemma." Paper read at the American Psychological Association, Los Angeles, August 1981.

Gilligan, C. "In a Different Voice: Women's Conceptions of Self and of Morality." *Harvard Educational Review,* 1977, *47* (4), 4–517.

Heist, P., and Yonge, G. *Omnibus Personality Inventory, Form F Manual.* New York: The Psychological Corporation, 1962.

Hochbaum, J. "Structure and Process in Higher Education." *College and University,* 1968, *43,* 190–202.

Hyatt, S. A. "Facilities Planning for Academic Results." *Planning for Higher Education,* 1980, *9* (December), 10–13.

Jeanotte, L. D. "A Study of the Contributing Factors Relating to Why Indian Students Drop Out of or Graduate from Educational Programs at the University of North Dakota." Paper read at American Educational Research Association, New York, March 1982.

Knefelkamp, L., Widick, C., and Parker, C. *Applying New Development Findings.* New Directions for Student Services, no. 4. San Francisco: Jossey-Bass, 1978.

Kohlberg, L. J. "Stages of Moral Development." In C. M. Beck, B. S. Crittendan, and E.V. Sullivan (Eds.), *Moral Education.* Toronto: University of Toronto Press, 1971.

Krathwohl, D. R., Bloom, B. S., and Masia, B. B. *Taxonomy of Educational Objectives. Handbook II: Affective Domain.* New York: McKay, 1964.

Lasch, C. *The Culture of Narcissism: American Life in an Age of Diminishing Expectations.* New York: Norton, 1978.

Lenning, O. T., Munday, L. A., Johnson, O. B., Vander Well, A. R., and Bruce, E. J. *The Many Faces of College Success and Their Nonintellective Correlates.* Monograph 15. Iowa City, Iowa: American College Testing Program, 1974

Lenning, O. T., Sauer, K., and Beal, P. E. *Student Retention Strategies. AAHE-ERIC Higher Education Research Report No. 8.* Iowa City, Iowa: American College Testing Program, 1980.

Levine, A. *When Dreams and Heroes Died: A Portrait of Today's College Student.* San Francisco: Jossey-Bass, 1980.

Morrill, R. *Teaching Values in College: Facilitating Development of Ethical, Moral, and Value Awareness in Students.* San Francisco: Jossey-Bass, 1980.

Naisbitt, J. *Megatrends: Ten New Directions Transforming Our Lifes.* New York: Warner, 1982.

Newcomb, T. "The Nature of Peer Group Influence." In T. M. Newcomb and E. K. Wilson (Eds.), *College Peer Groups.* Chicago: Aldine, 1966.

Pace, C. R., and Stern, G. G. "An Approach to the Measurement of Psychological Characteristics of College Environments." *Journal of Educational Psychology,* 1958, *49,* 269–277.

Pascarella, E. T., and Terenzini, P. T. "Patterns of Student-Faculty Informal Inter-action Beyond the Classroom and Voluntary Freshman Attrition." *Journal of Higher Education,* 1977, *48,* 540–552.

Perry, W. G., Jr. *Forms of Intellectual and Ethical Development in College.* New York: Holt, Rinehart and Winston, 1970.

Pettus, J. P. "Psychological Androgyny: Construct Validation and Relationship to Mental Health and Sex Stereotpyes." Unpublished doctoral dissertation, University of Montana, 1976.

Ramist, L. "College Student Attrition and Retention." *College Board Report No. 80-1.* Princeton, N.J.: College Entrance Examination Board, 1981.

Selye, H. *Stress Without Distress.* New York: Signet, 1975.

Simpson, C., Baker, K., and Mellinger, G. "Conventional Failures and Unconven-tional Dropouts: Comparing Different Types of University Withdrawals." *Sociology of Education,* 1980, *53,* 203–214.

Suchinsky, R. T. "Psychological Characteristics of the 1980s College Student: An Exploration of the Psychologic Process Involved in the Development of Narcissistic Character Patterns." *NASPA Journal,* 1982, *19* (4), 13–25.

Terenzini, P. T., and Pascarella, E. T. "Student-Faculty Contacts and Freshman Year Educational Outcomes, A Replication." Paper read at the Association for Institutional Research, San Diego, May 1979.

Terenzini, P. T., Pascarella, E. T., and Lorang, W. G. "An Assessment of the Academic and Social Influences on Freshman Year Educational Outcomes." *Review of Higher Education,* 1982, *5* (Winter), 86–110.

Trent, J. W., and Medsker, L. L. *Beyond High School.* San Francisco: Jossey-Bass, 1968.

University of California. "University of California Undergraduate Enrollment Study." *Report of the Task Group on Retention and Transfer.* Berkeley: University of California, 1980.

Upcraft, M. L., Peterson, P. C., and Moore, B. L. *The Academic and Extracurricular Expe-riences of Penn State Students.* Unpublished manuscript, Pennsylvania State Univer-sity, 1981a.

Upcraft, M. L., Peterson, P. C., and Moore, B. L. *The Academic and Personal Development of Penn State Freshmen.* University Park: Pennsylvania State University, 1981b.

Upcraft, M. L., and Pilato, G. T. *Residence Hall Assistants in College.* San Francisco: Jossey-Bass, 1982.

Warren, J. *The Measurement of Academic Competence.* Berkeley, Calif.: Educational Testing Service, 1978.

Western Interstate Commission for Higher Education. *The Ecosystem Model: Designing Campus Environments.* Boulder, Colo.: Western Interstate Commission for Higher Education, 1973.

Winter D. G., McClelland, D. C., and Stewart, A. J. "Understanding the Effects of 'Ivy College': An Integrated Model." In D. G. Winter, D. C. McClelland, and A. J. Stewart (Eds.), *Liberal Arts: Assessing Institutional Goals and Student Development.* San Francisco: Jossey-Bass, 1981.

M. Lee Upcraft is director of Counseling and Health Services of Pennsylvania State University and a member of the graduate faculty.

Joni E. Finney is an assistant director of Residence Hall Programs at Pennsylvania State University, with a special interest in women's concerns.

Peter Garland is an assistant director of Residence Hall Programs at Pennsylvania State University and a doctoral student in higher education, with a special interest in societal issues.

Orientation planners must understand the definition, goals, components, rationale, and methodologies of a comprehensive and effective program.

Orientation Programs and Activities

M. Lee Upcraft
William Michael Farnsworth

If we are to develop orientation programs and activities that enhance retention and personal development, they must be developed in a well thought out, planned way. This chapter offers a definition of and rationale for orienting entering students. We will review the basic goals and components of a comprehensive orientation program, suggest several methodologies for delivering orientation programs, and discuss the evaluation of orientation programs.

Definition and Rationale

Orientation is any effort on the part of an institution to help entering students make the transition from their previous environment to the collegiate environment and to enhance their success in college. Although orientation programs and services may vary in scope, purpose, length, timing, and content, most institutions give some initial attention to entering students. Typical efforts include providing information to entering students about facilities, programs, and services of

M. L. Upcraft (Ed.). *Orienting Students to College.* New Directions for
Student Services, no. 25. San Francisco: Jossey-Bass, March 1984.

the institution and giving them the opportunity to meet faculty, staff, and other students.

Why bother with orienting entering students? If students are truly adults and responsible for their own education, isn't it the responsibility of entering students, not the institution, to make a successful transition to college? The answers to this question range from the philosophical to the practical. On the philosophical side, the argument is that institutions have an obligation to help entering students maximize their chances for succeeding in college. An institution should care enough about its students to provide them the best possible opportunity to attain their educational goals, get good grades, and graduate from college. Getting off to a good start is important in this effort.

On the practical side, in an era of declining enrollments, many institutions are stepping up their efforts to recruit and retain students. There is considerable recent evidence that orientation programs help retain students, from summer preenrollment programs through programs and services offered upon arrival to the campus (Lenning, Sauer, and Beal, 1980; Ramist, 1981; Beal and Noel, 1980; University of California, 1980). It is in the best interest of the institution as well as the entering student to provide orientation programs and services.

Orientation Goals

What should the goals of orientation programs and services be? First, and foremost, orientation programs should help students with their academic adjustment to college. This results in maximum academic achievement and retention. Entering students should be familiar with academic requirements and be able to make a realistic assessment of their ability to meet these requirements. They should learn about the academic demands of the classroom and how to study and learn in that environment. They should know the breadth and depth of the academic offerings of the institution and be aware of both the academic support services available and the opportunities for intellectual development.

Second, orientation programs and services should help students with their personal adjustment to college. This results in maximum personal development. Entering students should be aware of the developmental issues they are likely to encounter in college (see Chapter One). They should learn how active participation in the living and learning environment of the campus can help them with these issues. They should also know about the student support services available to help students with problems and concerns.

Third, orientation programs and services should help the families of entering students understand what their sons, daughters, or spouses are about to experience. Families need to know the academic and personal adjustments entering students must make; more important, they need to know how support, advice, and encouragement can make a difference in the success of their loved ones.

Fourth, orientation programs and services should help the institution learn more about its entering students. It is as important for the faculty and staff of an institution to understand its entering students as it is for students to understand the institution. Orientation programs and services can provide information to faculty and staff about entering students and can provide an opportunity for students and faculty to get to know one another. There is substantial evidence that students who develop relationships with faculty are more likely to succeed in college than those who do not (Magnarella, 1979; Pascarella and Terenzini, 1980).

Orientation Components

Orientation goals must be translated into programs and services that serve entering students, their families, and the collegiate community. First and foremost, orientation must be a sustained and coordinated effort. It must begin at the time of admission and continue throughout the first year of enrollment. Orientation can be divided into three phases: preenrollment, initial enrollment, and the rest of the first year. Institutions must provide information and programs before students enroll, during the first few days on the campus, and throughout the first year of enrollment.

Second, orientation must have the support and involvement of the entire campus community, including faculty, staff, students, and especially the central administration. They must all understand the importance of orientation to the adjustment and success of entering students and provide appropriate support through participation and contribution of resources.

Third, orientation must be based on sound concepts of student development and on what is known about the influence of the collegiate environment. Orientation should also be based on all available information about entering students, including their backgrounds, academic abilities, interests, and needs. Often, the information is collected by the admissions office but never makes its way to orientation planners. Such information can be extremely valuable in fitting orientation programs to the needs of entering students.

Fourth, orientation must use a wide variety of interventions, including media approaches; group programming; academic courses; and individual tutoring, advising, and counseling. Each of these techniques will be elaborated later in this chapter. Orientation planners must not be restricted to traditional interventions such as group programs. They must use every effective means available to meet entering students' needs.

Fifth, orientation must be appropriately timed and sequenced from the preenrollment period, through the entering period, to the post-entering period. Too often, orientation planners overwhelm students with anything and everything they might need to know. Orientation planners must not only decide what entering students need to know, but when they need to know it and in what dosages. That is not an easy task. Deciding what to do before students enroll, while they enroll, and after they enroll should be based on their readiness to receive information.

Sixth, orientation must be evaluated to determine if it is effective. The relationship between orientation programs and orientation goals must be determined. Does orientation, in fact, help academic achievement and retention? Does it help in personal development? Are families of entering students helped? Do faculty and staff better understand their entering students? This information is crucial to determine whether students have been helped as well as to meet institutional goals.

Finally, orientation must be coordinated by a central office or person. The orientation program must be staffed by well-qualified professional educators and administrators who know and understand all aspects of orienting entering students and who have the administrative skills to build an effective program.

Effective Orientation Methodologies

No one method of implementing orientation programs can fulfill all the goals of orientation. Therefore, a wide variety of methods must be used. We recommend several methods, including (1) visual and written media; (2) academic courses; (3) group programs and activities; and (4) individual counseling, advising, and tutorial interventions.

Media. Most orientation publications provide an accurate reflection of the immediate concerns of entering students as well as of many of their developmental needs. Typically, these publications are distributed to entering students before their arrival on campus or during the first few days of residence. Although the format and writing styles of these publications differ dramatically, the content is relatively consistent.

Many of these publications begin with a welcome from a high-ranking university administrator, a student government leader, or those responsible for orientation programs. These brief statements convey messages like the following: We're glad you chose our respective institution; we realize you are new to this community and have special needs; we are ready, willing, and able to help; we have a few tips on how to achieve success; and we wish you the best of luck.

These publications also include specific instructions about arrival day, including campus traffic patterns, parking and unloading vehicles, room check-in procedures, and luggage and trunk storage information. They also identify university staff who are available on opening day to help students and parents. Information about student housing is also discussed, including room assignments, room change procedures, room furnishings, common facilities, temporary housing arrangements, residence hall security, special interest housing, and telephone and postal services. Entering students living elsewhere are provided with information concerning landlord-tenant responsibilities such as leasing arrangements, damage lists, escalator clauses, subletting, and security deposits. There may also be helpful hints about consumer issues such as grocery and used furniture shopping, checking accounts, utility hook-up procedures, energy conservation, telephone service, and automobile maintenance. Telephone numbers for local police, fire, ambulance, and health services are also contained in these orientation publications.

Available modes of transportation to, from, and around the campus are often explained and campus and community maps included. In an effort to familiarize entering students with their new environment, tours of the campus and surrounding community, highlighting special points of interest, are scheduled and announced in these publications. Calendars are also frequently included. These contain information about the dates, times, and places of important events or occurrences, including arrival day schedules; chronological listings of orientation programs and activities, sports, and cultural events; important academic dates such as drop-add periods, mid-term and final exam dates, registration, and course withdrawal periods; and traditional campus activities such as homecoming or parent's weekend.

Once these basic information needs have been addressed, orientation publications often discuss entering students' developmental needs. Since entering students include several unique student groups such as transfer students, minorities, returning adult students, disabled students and traditional students, orientation publications may provide a discussion of their unique needs and interests.

Entering students can often find useful advice about survival and success during the first year at college. The fundamental message is that academic success is dependent upon nonacademic variables as well as academic ones. Entering students are frequently advised to initiate and maintain meaningful relationships with peers, faculty, and staff; to develop personal interests and become involved in campus activities; to be sensitive to the changing dynamics between them and their parents; and to be cautious concerning the amount of time devoted to outside employment while being a new student. They are advised to work as hard at life outside the classroom as they do at life inside the classroom.

Academic skills are often discussed in orientation publications, including becoming efficient and effective at reading college-level texts, taking exams, preparing research papers, managing time, and making important decisions. Because information on academic skills is usually limited, students are encouraged to use special tutorial or support services for further help.

In order to help entering students establish contacts with faculty, orientation publications typically provide information about the faculty and their instructional, research, and public service roles. Formal academic advising relationships are mentioned along with the importance of nurturing informal out-of-class relationships. Sometimes entering students are warned that advisers and students don't always hit it off; these publications often suggest ways in which students might handle this problem.

Often the organizational hierarchy of the college is described so that entering students understand the lines of authority and responsibility that exist between various faculty and administrative positions. From the graduate assistant to the department head to the dean, students are told how to use these people to deal with the typical problems and concerns of the classroom.

A description of student support services is found in most orientation publications. Health services, career development and placement services, student activities, residential life programs, religious affairs, counseling services, learning assistance centers, and other services are introduced to entering students. Their use is strongly encouraged. Sometimes financial aid offices will present information concerning aid application deadlines, available scholarships, aid eligibility, and award dates.

In addition to publications for entering students, some institutions offer special orientation publications for parents. These publications often include a brief history of the institution; a statement of its mission; a review of the personal adjustment factors experienced by new students; an explanation of the organizational hierarchy; a review of the university budget; information about financial issues such as tuition, room and board cost, payment plans, and a typical student budget; and academic grading procedures.

For the most part, audiovisual presentations prepared for entering students present the same information contained in orientation publications. An audiovisual presentation, when well done, can be an effective means of delivering information but is not an end in and of itself. Their use should be augmented by opportunities for discussion with appropriate personnel.

Orientation Courses. Many institutions extend and sustain their orientation efforts through required or optional academic courses. Orientation courses are a means of helping entering students benefit not only from what they have been told in advance of enrollment but also from what they experience after enrollment. For example, it is one thing to stress the challenge of increased academic competition to an entering student and quite another to help that student deal with competition as it is experienced for the first time. Institutions that offer orientation courses may enhance retention, academic performance, and use of student support services. They may also ensure a quicker adjustment to and better understanding of the institution and a more positive attitude about the teaching-learning process.

Most orientation courses encompass the following goals:

1. To encourage entering students to examine the purposes of higher education and to develop their educational goals.
2. To help entering students learn about campus facilities, programs, and services.
3. To provide entering students with an opportunity to compare and contrast their experiences with other students.
4. To make entering students more aware of the issues and problems encountered during the first year of enrollment.
5. To provide entering students with some insight into their academic and personal needs and the collegiate environment in which they live.
6. To help entering students select courses according to class and load, difficulty, areas of interest, and applicability to future plans.
7. To inform entering students about the university policies, rules, regulations, and procedures that govern campus life.

8. To provide entering students with an opportunity to interact closely with at least one member of the faculty or staff.
9. To help entering students explore possible career goals.
10. To teach entering students relevant academic skills such as writing, research, discussion techniques, and study skills.
11. To provide faculty with an up-to-date understanding of entering students' needs and concerns.

There are a wide variety of teaching strategies used in teaching such orientation courses. Listed below are some highly desirable teaching and learning strategies, which may be effective in developing optimal learning conditions (Gardner, 1978).

1. Visits and exposure to many campus resources and facilities.
2. Class speakers such as university officials, community leaders, or even an occasional member of the board of trustees.
3. Class field trips to campus points of interest and selected aspects of the surrounding city.
4. Class discussions on topics of mutual interest and assigned topics.
5. Peer teaching on subjects about which students have expertise.
6. An introduction to the professor's own discipline.
7. "Getting to know you" exercises.
8. Values and clarification exercises.
9. Communication skills and listening skills exercises.
10. Group problem-solving exercises oriented toward common problems students experience in adjusting to the university.
11. Class attendance at lectures, debates, programs, and other events.
12. Individual and group projects.
13. Reading, writing, research, and discussion assignments.

Several institutions offer orientation courses, but the program at the University of South Carolina is probably the best known and most well developed. Other institutions that offer orientation courses include Penn State University, University of Georgia, Southern Illinois at Carbondale, University of Delaware, Florida State University, Southern Connecticut State College, Clarion State College, Marietta College, Brandywine College, and many others.

Group Programs and Activities. There are thousands of group orientation programs and activities that occur at the beginning of the academic year. Some are designed to meet such immediate maintenance needs of entering students as becoming familiar with the geography of the campus; locating important resources such as the bookstore, cafeteria, classrooms, and student support services, businesses, and governmental services. Other programs are designed to meet developmental needs, with particular focus on interpersonal and academic needs such as those presented in Chapter One.

Social programs often dominate group programs and activities, especially during the first few days of enrollment. These are important because they allow entering students to meet and greet one another and upper class students, thus meeting an important developmental need. But they also give rise to the frequent criticism of orientation programs — that they are just fun and games, with little or no educational substance. If, however, social programs are but one part of a comprehensive developmental programming effort, they are more likely to be seen as having educational value.

By offering programs that cover the breadth of entering students' development needs, institutions can build educational substance into their orientation efforts. The 1980 National Orientation Directors Association (NODA) Data Bank is an extremely helpful resource guide for programs offered at specified institutions which cover all the developmental needs identified in Chapter One. A few examples follow, but the reader is strongly encouraged to refer to the NODA Data Bank for specific programs.

Academic and intellectual development programs include seminars on current critical issues by distinguished faculty, academic fairs, classroom simulations, registration simulations, study skills workshops, group academic advising, and social gatherings with faculty. Interpersonal relations programs include adventure training, assertiveness training, roommate relationships, and big brother–big sister programs. Sexuality programs include women's awareness seminars; peer contraceptive education programs; and programs on dating, sexually transmitted diseases, and sexual values. Career development programs include opportunities to identify, reaffirm, or change career choices and professional interest forums to help entering students establish contact with practicing professionals who are in a career chosen by, or of interest to, entering students. Personal health and wellness programs include alcohol awareness programs, nutrition information sessions, weight control programs, and intramural sports orientations. Philosophy of life programs include seminars by campus or community clergy, values clarification programs, and discussions of current social issues.

Counseling, Advising, and Tutoring Interventions. Sometimes the best way to help entering students is on a one-to-one basis. Students are encouraged to seek out their academic adviser, resident assistant, financial aid counselor, career counselor, or other person to help with a problem or assist in initial adjustment. Comprehensive orientation programs should make use of the many individuals who can help students. This one-to-one assistance may be especially important to nonmainstream students such as transfers; returning adults; or minority students who may feel, rightly or wrongly, that media, courses, and group programs do not meet their needs.

Institutions have a responsibility to make sure that the individuals to whom students are referred are skilled in dealing with their needs. It may be necessary to offer training programs for those dealing with entering students. Faculty may need special training to meet the unique needs of entering students, particularly those who are not mainstream. At some institutions, faculty are taught how to interpret test profiles and assist with course placement. Campuses that offer special services for nonmainstream students may want to encourage entering students to set up individual appointments with staff members specifically trained to discuss their unique problems and concerns.

Evaluation of Orientation Programs and Services

As stated earlier in this chapter, orientation must be evaluated to determine if programs and services meet orientation goals. There must be a demonstrable relationship between participation in orientation activities and entering students' academic achievement, retention, and personal development. There must also be some evidence that families knew and understood what sons, daughters, or spouses went through. Finally, there must be some evidence that the campus community learned about and understood its entering students.

Gathering this evidence is not always done. When it is done, the results are not always valid because of the limitations of this type of evaluation or because of poor research designs. Essentially, there are two evaluation techniques. The first is to ask entering students, their families, and the campus community if they think orientation programs and activities were effective and why. They can be asked what was valuable, what was a waste of time, and what improvements could be made. There should be a review of which programs were attended, which were not, and why. Evaluations can be made immediately after students participate in orientation programs or toward the end of the first year of enrollment. This information can be extremely valuable to orientation planners in deciding what should be done and when to do it. Orientation programs are not a success unless they are viewed as a success by entering students and their families, faculty, staff, and participating upper class students.

The second evaluation technique is a more thorough, comprehensive evaluation study in which the relationship between orientation participation and students' academic and personal development during the first year is analyzed. One type of study that is frequently reported is to compare drop-outs with persisters to determine if there are any differences in the level and extent of participation in orientation programs and activities. Another type of study is to compare entering students who participated in orientation with those who did not, controlling for appropriate background ability and personality factors to determine if there are any differences in academic achievement, retention, and personal development. There are quite a few of the former type of study (Lenning, Sauer, and Beal, 1980; Ramist, 1981; Beal and Noel, 1980; University of California, 1980) and almost none of the latter type. Both techniques are needed to determine the effectiveness of orientation programs and activities.

Summary

In this chapter we have offered a definition of and rationale for orientation programs for entering students. We have reviewed the basic goals of a comprehensive orientation, identified the methodologies of effective programs, and given several suggestions for orientation programming based on student need. We have also stressed the importance of institutional support and evaluation of orientation programs. Most important, we have tried to demonstrate the importance of orientation as a means of helping students succeed in college.

References

Beal, P. E., and Noel, L. *What Works in Student Retention.* Joint Project Report. Iowa City, Iowa: American College Testing Program and the National Center for Higher Education Management Systems, 1980.

Gardner, J., and others. "University 101: A Model for Student and Faculty Development." Paper presented at the conference of the Association of Higher Education, Chicago, March 1978.

Lenning, O. T., Sauer, K., and Beal, P. E. "Student Retention Strategies." *AAHE-ERIC Higher Education Research Report No. 8.* Washington, D.C.: American Association of Higher Education, 1980.

Magnarella, P. J. "The Continuing Evaluation of a Living-Learning Center." *Journal of College Student Personnel,* 1979, *20,* 4–9.

Pascarella, E. T., and Terenzini, P. T. "Student-Faculty and Student-Peer Relationships as Mediators of the Structural Effects of Undergraduate Residence Arrangement." *Journal of Educational Research,* 1980, *73* (July/August), 344–353.

Ramist, L. *College Student Attrition and Retention. College Board Report, no. 80-81.* Princeton, N.J.: College Entrance Examination Board, 1981.

38

Simpson, C., Baker, K., and Mellinger, G. "Conventional Failures and Unconventional Dropouts: Comparing Different Types of University Withdrawals." *Sociology of Education*, 1980, *53* (October), 203–214.

University of California. *University of California Undergraduate Enrollment Study*. Report of the Task Group on Retention and Transfer. Berkeley: University of California, 1980.

M. Lee Upcraft is director of Counseling and Health Services of Pennsylvania State University and a member of the graduate faculty.

William Michael Farnsworth is assistant director of Residential Life Programs for New Student Programs at Pennsylvania State University and directs a comprehensive orientation program designed to meet the needs of all entering students.

A wide variety of interventions and strategies must be used to meet the needs of traditional, eighteen-year-old, just-out-of-high-school, entering students.

Orienting Traditional Entering Students

Betty L. Moore
Patricia C. Peterson
J. Robert Wirag

The need for special efforts to ease the transition from home to college has long been recognized. Consequently, most orientation programs are designed to meet the needs of late adolescent, mainstream, entering students. In this chapter we will describe the unique needs of traditional entering students who are eighteen years old, have just completed high school, and are enrolling in college for the first time. We will offer suggestions for programs and services to meet their needs, based on the developmental model presented in Chapter One.

Needs of Traditional Entering Students

In some ways, traditional entering students are the same as other entering students. They are worried most about whether they will succeed academically and whether they will find friends and groups with which to affiliate. They worry about becoming familiar with the geography of the campus, locating important offices and classrooms, and finding out about local and community services and facilities. Like

M. L. Upcraft (Ed.). *Orienting Students to College.* New Directions for
Student Services, no. 25. San Francisco: Jossey-Bass, March 1984.

other entering students, they are anxious about their ability to make it in college and the newness of an environment that may be threatening.

Unlike returning adult students or transfers, many traditional entering students will be on their own for the first time, free of parental and community influence and restrictions. Even those living at home will seek a freer, more autonomous, less restricted relationship with their parents. They will be establishing themselves as autonomous human beings, achieving independence from childhood influences and, for the first time, assuming responsibility for their lives. They will vacillate from dependence to independence, in part because most of them will still be economically, if not emotionally, dependent upon their parents. They will learn that freedom involves responsibility and that responsibility is not always an easy burden to carry. They will become more aware of who they are, both intellectually and emotionally. Achieving independence and autonomy and establishing a clearer sense of identity are an important part of the development of traditional entering students.

Traditional entering students are also late adolescents, with all of their need to affiliate and identify with one another. There is ample evidence that the peer group is an especially powerful influence on traditional students' lives, mostly because they have a need to replace family and community support systems with peer support systems. Because of their common backgrounds, interests, personality characteristics, and goals, and because as entering students they are all in the same boat, they have a strong need to be liked and accepted by one another and to influence and be influenced by one another. The late adolescent peer group provides norms and behavior guidelines that are enforced through direct rewards and punishments. As a result, traditional entering students are more likely to transfer some control over themselves to the group and become subject to its influence.

It might be helpful, however, to look more specifically at the experiences of the typical late adolescent during the first few days of college. For residential students, away from home for the first time, college begins with the ritualistic and sometimes traumatic farewell to parents. There is also the fear and excitement of meeting a new roommate, wondering who this person is and if they will get along. There is the fear that somehow they are not like everyone else and the assumption that no one else could be as scared and awkward as they are. There may even be an exaggerated effort to appear confident, cool, and experienced, in spite of feeling unconfident, scared, and inexperienced. The first few days are filled with excitement, experimentation, new experiences, and missing home and family.

For commuting students, there may be expectations that living at home will somehow be different now that they are in college. Those expectations may or may not work out. Parents may still want to retain some regulatory functions in spite of their child's new status as a college student. Commuting students may feel out of it because they are living at home and may think they are missing a lot by not living on campus. They may be trying to figure out how they can become more a part of campus life, trying to learn more about where to hang out between classes to meet new people. On the other hand, they still may have several friends from high school around. The first few days are filled with uncertainty about how to fit in and how to establish an identity as a student and an adult, while living at home.

The combination of being on their own for the first time, and being especially subject to the influence of their peers cannot be forgotten in planning orientation programs and services for traditional entering students. Programs should contain special topics to meet these needs and should capitalize on peer group support and influence to reinforce whatever learning is planned.

It is especially important to offer programs and services for traditional entering students in some developmental sequence. According to Maslow (1954), a person cannot attend to higher level needs when basic needs are not yet met. Maslow's hierarchy of needs, from lowest to highest are: (1) physiological needs—basic bodily needs for sleep, food, stimulation, or activity; (2) safety needs—protection against bodily harm or injury and security against threat; (3) belongingness and love needs—acceptance, affection, approval, and warmth; (5) esteem needs—self-respect, status, and worth; and (5) self-actualization or fulfillment needs—development of full individuality and realization of potential (Maslow, 1968). The sick student who can't find the Health Center won't care much about attending a values seminar. The entering student who does not feel some acceptance and approval from others is not likely to be interested in a career development workshop.

Not all entering students have precisely the same needs at the same time. A well-balanced orientation program will include offerings targeted at various levels of the needs hierarchy. The first few days of orientation should target the more basic needs such as physiological needs, safety needs, and belongingness. Later in the orientation week and throughout the year, the balance should shift to higher level needs such as belongingness, esteem, and self-actualization.

Programs to Meet Immediate Needs

Traditional entering students need to become familiar with the physical setting of the campus and be assured that safety and security needs will be met. They also need to get acquainted with other entering students and to deal with academic worries and concerns. The following examples, as well as other examples offered throughout this chapter, are drawn from the National Orientation Directors Association *Data Bank*, 1980.

Becoming familiar with the physical setting can be achieved through creative maps highlighting usage of resources and through organized tours of important facilities such as the library, the bookstore, and the health center. Examples of innovative tours include bicycle tours led by faculty at Skidmore College, roller skating through campus at the University of Michigan, and a scavenger hunt devised by Bradley University as another way to help students develop a personal map of their new environment. Safety and security needs can be approached through (1) distributing pamphlets on bike regulations and registration, police services, and emergency resource numbers; (2) requiring a tour of the health center; (3) discussing dorm floor security; and (4) reviewing safety measures while walking on campus at night. Western New England College has a separate orientation program specifically focused on such safety and security needs.

Getting acquainted activities may include audiovisual, multimedia presentations and videotaped slide shows that inform entering students about various aspects of their physical environment and, indirectly, about some of the important social norms — such activities occur at Lander College, Penn State University, Muskegon Community College, and Salisbury State College. These presentations often run continuously on a self-initiated signal or are linked to small group discussions which might include parents as well as entering students. The Dial Direct Telephone Tape System, which has been inaugurated at the University of Maryland, Penn State University, and the State University of New York at Buffalo, is another useful orientation medium.

Making a satisfactory academic adjustment is high on the list of immediate needs for most incoming students (Higginson, Moore, and White, 1981). Orientation should inform students about choosing a major; registration procedures; course selection and scheduling; academic survival techniques such as study skills, test taking, handling academic stress, and evaluating local academic competition; and locating key academic resources. An area of academic development often overlooked by orientation planners is information about honor societies: how they can motivate entering students by informing them about special honor courses and department options and give them a sense of the relationship between academic success and future career goals.

Programs to Meet Developmental Needs

Chapter One identifies and describes the developmental issues of entering students. Since a majority of these are traditional, eighteen-year-old, entering students, we will briefly highlight their unique developmental needs and present examples of programs and activities that meet those needs.

Developing Intellectual and Academic Competence. Ask traditional entering students what they fear most about coming to college and most will say, "flunking out." Very few students fresh out of high school realize that success in college can be something more than earning good grades. With the possible exception of those late adolescents who are attracted to prestigious institutions stressing intellectual development, most students come to college with a limited intellectual awareness. Through orientation programs, they can be introduced to the intellectual life of the campus, including the free discussion of ideas, the importance of openness and tolerance, the standards of logical and rational thought, the appreciation of the arts, the appreciation of learning for learning's sake, and the value of the search for truth.

It is sometimes argued that traditional entering students are more interested in fun and games in orientation than they are in intellectual development. On the contrary, late adolescents often complain that orientation programs lack intellectual substance and faculty participation. In addition to programs that help students adjust academically, programs must enhance intellectual development.

Programs that enhance intellectual and academic development often begin during the summer before enrollment. At this time, parents and students visit the campus, meet with various academic support personnel, review placement test profiles, put together a tentative schedule of courses, discuss academic requirements, and interact with faculty or deans of specific academic units. Programs such as these can be found at the University of Nebraska, Penn State University, San Diego State University, Dominican College, Seminole Community College, Mansfield State College, University of Maryland, and Michigan State University.

Advising activities also occur immediately preceding the academic term and sometimes continue throughout the first semester or first year — Adams State College in Colorado, University of Arizona, Elmhurst College in Illinois, University of South Carolina, Reinhardt in Georgia, and University of Utah are examples. Other approaches include academic exploration fairs offering information on different majors, the opportunity for new students to meet faculty from the various departments, videotapes on requirements of various major fields, information on the college grading system, and an overview of the class period schedule and academic procedures — these approaches are used at Albion College in Michigan, Pacific Lutheran College, and Salisbury State College in Maryland.

Sessions that teach students how to register can help them handle the stress, confusion, crowds, and harried decisions of academic registration. At some colleges, faculty hold miniclasses, last lecture series, or simulated lab periods to acclimate students to the academic environment — C. W. Post Center of Long Island University, University of Guelph in Canada, and North Carolina State are examples of this approach. Academic courses for credit are offered on a regular basis throughout the first semester or first year on such topics as cultural orientation at the University of Southern California, human potential at Lurleen Wallace Junior College in Alabama, communication skills in relation to adjusting to college life at Robert Morris College in Illinois, student development seminars at San Antonio College, academic enrichment at the University of Utah, exploration in human relations at West Chester State College, and decision making at Penn State University. Honor societies and other scholarly options available to entering students should also be highlighted.

Study skills workshops by student counselors or advisers (at Penn State University) or faculty (at C. W. Post Center of Long Island University), along with general discussions about academic adjustment and survival given by the University of Massachusetts, Otterbein College of Ohio, or Salem State help entering students meet academic expectations and handle academic competition. At Penn State University, student counselors are available at the request of resident assistants, fraternities and sororities, and club advisers to help to teach entering students time management, study methods, note taking, and test-taking techniques.

As we previously stressed, programs promoting intellectual and academic development should go beyond study skills, miniregistrations, and exploration fairs. Orientation is an opportunity to encourage entering students to discuss critical topics, participate in the intellectual life of the campus, and interact with faculty. Penn State University, the University of Delaware, and other institutions offer entering students an opportunity to enhance their intellectual and academic development through special residential programs. Students are assigned to houses according to academic interests, programs are developed that promote scholarly and academic topics, and faculty are frequent participants in the life of the residence hall.

One traditional approach used by Cornell University and other institutions is to assign specific readings over the summer to be discussed by faculty and entering students. Cornell also includes a special section of orientation called "Beyond Orientation Week," which calls attention to cultural events scheduled throughout the year. Entering students should be encouraged to attend art exhibits, musical events, campus plays, and other activities. These activities may also have the side effect of getting faculty involved in orientation. Faculty participation helps promote the academic and intellectual tone of orientation programs. There is evidence that programs in which faculty participate have a favorable impact on the intellectual development of students (Upcraft, Peterson, and Moore, 1981).

Establishing and Maintaining Interpersonal Relationships. "What will my roommate be like?" "Will I find new friends to replace my old ones?" "Can I find new friends if I live at home?" These are questions entering students typically ask themselves as they anticipate college. Entering students who decide to leave college give reasons like, "I really missed my friends back home," or "I was so lonely at college I couldn't stand it any more." As pointed out in Chapter One, one of the most frequently mentioned worries of entering students is finding new friends.

Getting acquainted activities are geared toward helping entering students find friends to replace those left behind. These activities range from Playfair or New Games — found at King's College, Penn State University, University of Wisconsin, and SUNY at Pottsdam — to overnight campouts or retreats — at Taylor University, California State University, Northern Michigan University, and Georgia State University — to ice cream socials, "jammies," and coffee houses. At Penn State University, all freshmen are urged to complete a roommate starter kit (Peterman, Sagaria, and Sellers, 1977) which is designed to help roommates discuss topics that will help them get along. These topics include background information, personal attitudes, habits, and moods. Kansas Newman College holds a roommate retention workshop to facilitate roommate compatibility.

Entering students must also find others who share common interests and enthusiasms. An orientation program that meets this need is an activity fair where members of various sports and social groups, student services, student government, clubs, fraternities, and sororities display posters, run slide shows, hand out information sheets, or exhibit scrap books. The University of the District of Columbia has an activity fair, Texas Tech University has an activities carnival, Georgia State University has a market place, and Penn State University has "Horizons." Bradley University has a computer program linking entering students' activities, options, and interests. California State University sends out a special mailing during the summer to entering students, entitled *Belonging*, with information on the value of social participation.

Other interpersonal development activities that help entering students include being escorted by upper class students to faculty homes for dessert and discussion — this is done at the University of

California at Riverside, Pacific Lutheran University, and Springfield College. Penn State University has the UPclose Program in which small groups of students and faculty or staff visit a campus facility or hike through the countryside, meet over dinner, attend films, or participate in folk singing or a sports event.

Many orientation efforts recognize the continued importance of parents and indirectly serve young students by informing their parents about the physical campus, academic requirements, local norms, general collegiate enthusiasm, student services, as well as about their new roles as parents of a college student. Parents are offered campus and community tours at the University of Pittsburgh at Johnstown, open discussions led by professional staff on adjustment issues at Slippery Rock State College, introduction to college traditions at Hood College, student panels answering questions on college life at Notre Dame University, information about extracurricular activity opportunities at Slippery Rock State College, and meetings of parents with university personnel at North Carolina University and University of South Florida. Both Penn State University and Indiana University of Pennsylvania mail out *A Parent's Guide* magazine.

Finally, orientation programs should include some activities sponsored by the counseling staff on topics such as being more assertive, feeling comfortable socially, developing relationship skills, and handling homesickness. These programs may have to be marketed in a special way to attract participants, but even if fewer students show up than desired, the visibility of the offices providing these services is important.

Developing a Sex-Role Identity and Sexuality. It is unlikely that most late adolescents enter college asking themselves the question, "Who am I?" Yet "Who am I?" is a question frequently asked by entering students while experiencing the bumps and bruises of the first year. They may reconsider who they are as men and women and whether traditional sex-role stereotypes really fit. The new freedom of the collegiate environment may, for the first time, allow real choices about sexual activity. It would be a mistake to assume that most late adolescents, even if sexually active, know a lot about sex or the role of sexuality in relationships. Orientation programs must help them make choices about sex roles and sexual behavior.

Some of the interpersonal relations programs mentioned earlier may be helpful to the entering student in considering appropriate sexual behavior. But late adolescents need basic information about the biology of sex, birth control, and sexually transmitted diseases. This information is probably best presented by trained peers rather than counselors, health educators, or physicians. Penn State University, for example, has a very effective peer contraception education program using students trained by the University Health Center and cooperating with selected faculty.

In addition to information about basic sexuality, entering students must consider the implications of and their responsibility for their sexual activity. There should be opportunities to participate in programs that discuss the role of sexuality in a relationship and to consider the morality of sexual behavior. Faculty in psychology, sociology, health education, and human development can be valuable resources, as well as faculty in philosophy, religious studies, and related fields. Campus and community clergy can also be helpful in conducting these programs.

Programs on appropriate roles for men and women can also be valuable to entering students. These programs can range from discussions with faculty to those that allow entering students to grapple with sexual identity issues on a more personal level. Programs for women that raise awareness of women's issues such as equal employment opportunities, sex-based discrimination, careers and families, and sex-free roles may also be helpful to men. Women in nontraditional fields may need orientation programs to help them cope with classrooms that are predominantly male or with faculty who are not sympathetic to their career goals.

Deciding upon a Career and Life-Style. "What do you want to be when you grow up?" is a question that most children are asked at a very early age. Unfortunately, many late adolescents are no more in a position to answer that question than they were when they were five years old. The college experience allows them to answer that question on a more realistic basis than ever before and with more freedom than they had at home. Today's late adolescents are often more concerned about career choices than their predecessors and are extremely anxious about being undecided. Many declare a major with little knowledge of or experience with their chosen field because admitting indecision is socially unacceptable. Some students are at college because it offers a holding pattern. These students should be reassured that being undecided is all right, as long as they commit themselves to a period of self- and career exploration. Orientation offers an opportunity to initiate this exploration. Entering students should also understand that choosing a career involves more than a single decision and is, in fact, a process which will recur during college and after.

Many of the academic and intellectual programs discussed previously are relevant to career and life-style issues because there is a strong relationship between academic choices and future career goals. Specific programs during orientation may be geared toward certain student subgroups such as women engineers or premed students or may be focused on distinctive issues. Traditional eighteen-year-old entering students may have had limited experiences with pursuing information needed before making a major decision. Information about career development services, courses, library resources, and computerized self-exploration programs should be available and visible during orientation. For example, Northern Michigan University and Salem State College bring together staff from academic departments, placement and counseling centers, and advising units in a special program for undeclared majors. Penn State University offers a career exploration and decision-making course for those having trouble narrowing their choices.

The focus of many of these orientation activities is to help entering students who are anxious about finding the right career or choosing the right major. Orientation programs should encourage entering students to take some time to explore and should let them know that other students are also undecided. These programs should also identify the importance of being aware of their own skills, interests, and life-style priorities.

Opportunities to locate pertinent part-time employment, internships, and to interview alumni in various career fields should also be available to entering students. Life-style choices, decision-making skills, and goal-setting techniques might be combined in a workshop that demonstrates how to clarify objectives, generate alternatives, process information, evaluate options, weigh consequences, establish specific goals, and determine strategies to achieve objectives.

Maintaining Personal Health and Wellness. Many entering students drop out of college because they have burned out. College has proven more stressful and physically debilitating than they ever imagined. Daily decisions regarding activity levels, sleep, stress, foods, drugs, alcohol, and smoking can enhance or retard college success. Orientation is the time to introduce entering students to the concepts of personal health and wellness, based on the assumption that daily habits are directly related to health, that the body has limits that must be recognized, and that good habits can impede illness (Dunn, 1961).

The social structure on many campuses seems to nurture conflicting norms. Students are urged to be aware of personal appearance and to work at staying fit and in shape. On the other hand, students are often pressured into drinking and drug activities or often sustain themselves on a diet lacking in essential nutrients, all of which contradict goals of good health. The concept of wellness goes beyond emphasizing the responsibility of young students to be aware of the effect of their many daily decisions. Wellness emphasizes the interaction of mental, emotional, physical, and spiritual health. Wise health habits usually result in energy, confidence, and the ability to cope. Orientation discussions focused on these decisions may help late adolescents become aware of the importance of maintaining personal health and wellness.

Student interest in health-related programs and activities has grown by leaps and bounds in recent years. Students flock to programs on diet, exercise, meditation, massage, grooming, bulimia, sexuality, and alcohol. Campuses abound with joggers, tennis players, aerobic dancers, and athletic teams in action. There is considerable readiness by traditional entering students to attend orientation programs on human sexuality; fitness and weight control; self-care, including stress management, alcohol behavior, and smoking behavior; and nutrition.

The use of alcohol and drugs is of concern to many colleges and universities. Orientation programs should emphasize responsible decisions regarding drug and alcohol use as well as institutional accountability for abuse. Penn State University, the University of Massachusetts, and the University of Florida have comprehensive alcohol awareness programs using trained peer educators who can help entering students consider whether or not to drink — most are already drinking before they come to college — and if they choose to drink, how to do so responsibly. Campuses and community resources for alcohol abusers should be also identified.

In planning orientation programs for personal health and wellness, there is an opportunity to present ongoing programs as well as one-time introductions to topics. These programs should include campus health referral sources, including counselors, health educators, and community resources. Written materials and pamphlets on health issues, which can be distributed to entering students, are abundant. Finally, extensive use of trained peers is strongly recommended because of their instant credibility with late adolescents.

Developing an Integrated Philosophy of Life. Traditional entering students may, for the first time, be free to choose values and behaviors without parental influence. As pointed out in Chapter One, they may astonish their parents with new values, beliefs, and behaviors, or they may simply retain what they were taught at home. Whether they change or stay the same, they will undoubtedly have to reconsider what is right and wrong, their priorities in life, their religious and spiritual beliefs, and how they fit into the larger order of things.

Developing an integrated philosophy of life is not usually high on the list of traditional entering students' concerns. Unlike many other developmental issues, such as sex and study skills, entering students must be encouraged to attend values sessions, life priority discussions, or discussions of spiritual or religious issues. Examples of these types of programs include the Social Barometer, in which students respond to values decisions on a continuum and discuss the reasons for their choices. Wesley College offers a program to entering students on life-style decisions. The State University of New York at Stony Brook provides a program on the consequences of personal decisions. By far the most popular programs are values clarification seminars in which students learn about criteria for values, value indicators, and the valuing process (Smith, 1977). Morrill (1980) offers a comprehensive approach for values development in college. The reader is encouraged to review his model when preparing for values programs in orientation.

Summary

In this chapter we have identified the needs of the traditional, late adolescent, eighteen- to nineteen-year-old entering students who comprise a substantial portion of today's entering students. We have reviewed programs and activities that meet their immediate and developmental needs. Designing programs for traditional entering students is only half the battle; the other half is getting them to attend and participate. There is evidence that those students who most need programs and services are least likely to participate in them (Upcraft, Peterson, and Moore, 1981). Special efforts will make orientation programs highly visible and encourage students to attend.

Traditional entering students are a diverse group with a wide range of developmental needs. The challenge of orientation planners is to demonstrate to these students that participation in orientation will be helpful to them in pursuing their personal and educational goals.

References

Dunn, H. *High-Level Wellness*. Arlington, Va.: R. W. Beatty, 1961.

Higginson, L., Moore, L., and White, E. "A New Role for Orientation: Getting Down to Academics." *National Association of Student Personnel Association Journal*, 1981, *19*, 21–28.

Maslow, A. H. *Motivation and Personality*. New York: Harper & Row, 1954.

Morrill, R. *Teaching Values in College: Facilitating Development of Ethical, Moral, and Value Awareness in Students*. San Francisco: Jossey-Bass, 1980.

National Orientation Directors Association. *1980 Data Bank.* College Park, Md: National Orientation Directors Association, 1980.

Peterman, D., Sagaria, M. A., and Sellers, J. E. *The Roommate Starter Kit.* State College, Pa., privately published, 1977.

Smith, M. *A Practical Guide to Value Clarification.* La Jolla, Calif.: University Associates, 1977.

Upcraft, M. L., Peterson, P. C., and Moore, B. L. "The Academic and Personal Development of Penn State Freshmen." Unpublished manuscript ofPennsylvania State University, 1981.

Betty L. Moore is general counselor in the Student Assistance Center of Pennsylvania State University.

Patricia C. Peterson is director of Campus Life at Pennsylvania State University.

J. Robert Wirag is the director of the Student Health Service at the University of Arkansas.

Meeting the needs of minority students is more a matter of understanding and sensitivity to the historical and societal context within which these students attend college than a matter of special orientation programs and activities.

Orienting Minority Students

Doris J. Wright

Since the 1954 *Brown* v. *Topeka Board of Education* Supreme Court decision that desegregated public institutions of learning, increasing numbers of minority students have enrolled at predominantly white institutions of higher learning (Richmond, 1979). Although this trend is likely to continue in the long run, the trend over the next decade is toward stability or downturn of minority students enrolling in large universities (Sedlacek and Webster, 1977).

These "new" students, as coined by Cross (1971), have challenged college orientation programs to create culturally appropriate ways of meeting their needs. Entering minority students possess a world view, a frame of reference, and culture-specific learning needs different from traditional students. Unfortunately, entering minority students have scars from painful life events—a result of having sought an education within an economically oppressive, nonsupportive world. It will be more difficult for these students to succeed in college if they do not manage these life events early in their college experience.

Helping minority students' transition to college is the responsibility of the institution's orientation staff. This chapter identifies issues important to entering minority students, describes the background characteristics of these students within a historical context, and analyzes societal influences that affect them. Culturally specific develop-

M. L. Upcraft (Ed.). *Orienting Students to College.* New Directions for Student Services, no. 25. San Francisco: Jossey-Bass, March 1984.

mental needs of entering minorities are discussed as well as problems in defining those needs using traditional developmental theories. The relationship of college orientation activities to overall minority student retention is described and practical suggestions for orientation programs are discussed.

Historical Perspectives

Ethnic minority students have not gained full access to higher education today, especially to predominantly white institutions. During the 1960s and early 1970s, several events occurred that increased minority students' access to white institutions. Enrollment for blacks and Hispanics increased during the same time period. Thomas (1981) reported that during the 1970s black student enrollment increased far more rapidly than white college enrollment. Five significant historical events influenced enrollment increases for blacks and other minorities, including (1) the 1954 *Brown* v. *Topeka Board of Education* Supreme Court decision, (2) the Civil Rights Movement, (3) the Equality of Education (EEO) Report, (4) the 1965 Higher Education Act, and (5) the 1973 Adams decision (Thomas, 1981). Collectively, these events greatly affected minority student access to higher education. The result of these federal enactments and civil rights activities was the growth of federally funded programs designed to increase minority participation in higher education.

For example, the Higher Education Act of 1965 provided Basic Educational Opportunity Grants (BEOG) and other financial aid packages that supported minority enrollment. The Adams decision of 1973 was enacted by Congress to require certain states to desegregate their dual systems of higher education. This mandate gave blacks and other minorities an opportunity to pursue higher education in white institutions where they had been denied full access in the past.

Minority students could not attend college without substantial financial support. The federal government provided several programs, including:

1. *Institutional Aid Program* — Tribally-Controlled Community College and Strengthening Developing Institutions Programs.
2. *Student Financial Aid* — Pell Grants (formerly BEOG); College Work-Study Program; and National Direct Student Loans.
3. *Special Programs* (for access and persistence) — Upward Bound; Talent Search; and Educational Opportunity Centers (Astin, 1977).

4. *Professional Training and Human Resource Development*—Minority Biomedical Support; Indian Education Fellowships for Indian Students; and Prefreshmen Cooperative Education for Minorities and Indians.

Unfortunately, although these programs have opened access to higher education for thousands of minorities, full access has not been fully achieved. Astin (1977) argued that access extends beyond enrollment in an institution and must include other interventions to help students succeed in college. One important intervention is orientation, in which institutions help students make a successful transition from their previous environment to the collegiate environment. Thus, institutions must develop orientation programs and activities designed to address the unique needs of entering minority students.

Characteristics of Entering Minority Students

Entering minority students are from diverse cultural environments: the barrio; the reservation; the urban ghetto; the farm or migrant town; and, in recent years, all-white suburbia, in the case of upwardly mobile minority families. No single statement may be made about the environments from which entering minorities come. However, there may be several common life experiences and characteristics that bond members of these groups together.

The most obvious mutually shared experience is that of having been systematically oppressed within American society. While the tool of that oppression has varied from use of internment camps to legislated enslavement, the outcome has remained the same: Minorities have been restricted from full participation in American society, including higher education. Entering minority students arrive on the campus having shared this common experience.

Blacks, Hispanics, Asians, and American Indians believe in maintaining a strong sense of community within which norms, customs, values, and cultural traditions are collectively shared and reinforced. The importance of community to the minority individual has been documented in the literature (Sue and Sue, 1977; Baldwin, 1981; Richardson, 1981). For the minority person, self-identity must be defined within a community in which a sense of self, a realistic self-appraisal, and culture-specific leadership competencies are developed.

Related to this sense of community is the importance of family to the minority student. Maintaining close ties with the primary or extended family unit has been noted by educators and clinicians (Sue,

1981; Richardson, 1981). Certain activities may be initiated only after an examination of its potential outcome for the family has been made. The family is central to culture-specific development of self-identity of minority students; role modeling of appropriate adult roles; and communication of culture-specific norms, customs, and values. The family supports its students, generally, and assists in problem resolution.

Further, entering minority students may be the first family members to attend college, creating expectations that could support and strengthen self-identity. This can also lead to unrealistic beliefs causing frustration, anxiety, and subsequent failure. The pressure of being the first may be increased if other family members were not able to attend college because of racial bias or limited economic resources. Entering minority students do not come to college alone; the entire family enrolls vicariously. This fact must be recognized as institutions deal with entering minority students.

A fourth characteristic of entering minority groups is that they are not culturally homogeneous. Intragroup heterogeneity has been observed among blacks (Sue, 1981), Asians (Sue, 1981), and Hispanics (Ruiz, 1981). Tribal differences have been noted among Native American tribes and Alaska Aleutes (Richardson, 1981). Intragroup differences may include attitudinal, familial, economic, or social class distinctions. Developing activities that acknowledge the intragroup variations in beliefs and behavior can provide greater insight and understanding into minority student needs.

In addition, many entering minority students may be moving from an environment where there were significant numbers of minority peers to a setting where they have to cope with being the only one. Without significant minority peer group support, students may feel lonely and alienated and lose self-confidence. Unfortunately, many majority collegiate environments respond insensitively. For example, faculty may single out minority students for special attention because of their skin color or language differences. These students may be asked to speak on behalf of all minorities and may feel pressure to answer, even if they feel incompetent to do so, because of a fear of a negative evaluation.

In summary, ethnic minorities represent peoples whose historical beginnings may be varied, but who share the common experience of having been oppressed. Blacks or African-Americans; Hispanics— Chicanos, Mexican-Americans, Puerto Ricans, and Cubans; Asian-Americans—Chinese, Japanese, and Filipinos; and Native Americans— including Alaska Aleutes—have been denied full participation in American society and access to college.

When the uniqueness of entering minority students is taken into account by those responsible for orienting them, they may derive a strong sense of self-confidence and self-worth. They may be motivated to enhance their culture-specific learning competencies and personal life skills. Ultimately, they may increase their chances of college success. Thus, colleges must first recognize and understand minority characteristics and then create orientation activities taking these characteristics into account. It is the responsibility of all institutions to create activities and programs that challenge and support entering minority students.

Developmental Needs of Entering Minorities

Entering minority students come to college with most of the developmental needs identified in Chapter One. They are concerned about academic success, finding friends, and choosing the right career. But these developmental needs occur within a context that is different from traditional entering students. Current developmental theories — for example, Perry, Chickering, Erikson, and others — have failed to describe adequately how minority students' social climate influences their overall development.

Most current developmental theories seek to explain how college students progress through stages or achieve increasingly complex tasks. Most of these theories are based on Western notions of human behavior. As a result, they may not permit full understanding of entering minority students. These theories are limiting because they (1) fail to acknowledge the oppressive living conditions of minorities, (2) fail to acknowledge the relationship of culture-specific world views to development, (3) do not understand the mind-body assumptions of non-Western world views, and (4) fail to define development in a historical context (Sue and Sue, 1977; Nobles, 1980; Richardson, 1981; Sue, 1981). These factors may promote development and help achieve personal success and therefore need to be integrated in a definition of development for entering minority students.

Background, environmental, and personality characteristics provide a cultural context around which minority developmental needs are defined. Entering minority students may enter college less academically prepared than their fellow students due to biased public school experiences. They may have been rewarded in different ways for their learning efforts. They come to college not having been appropriately challenged or supported for intellectual achievement or personal growth. Entering minority students, particularly those who may be first-generation college students, may have received little of the mentoring or role modeling that has been shown to facilitate personal and intellectual development.

In some instances entering minority students may have received challenging activities, support activities, and mentoring, but only in socially sanctioned areas such as athletics and music. It is likely that these growth activities failed to generalize into other developmental areas of the student's life, such as academic achievement and career aspirations. As a result, entering minority students may be starved for the challenge and support activities necessary for optimum growth. Capitalizing on this readiness is essential to motivate minority students early in their college experience. A balance of challenge and support activities is critical. Too much challenge without appropriate support activities may be perceived as negative and may limit the developmental process resulting in student attrition. Entering minorities need activities and programs in which they feel supported and valued before they are ready to accept more risky and challenging experiences. Orientation can help entering students recognize that it is possible to succeed on a predominantly white campus. However, success will require acceptance of the social and political realities of the campus. To achieve this goal, several developmental tools may become essential for the entering minority student.

First, entering minority students must realize the historical context through which their access to college was achieved. Learning how their ancestors sought to gain access may help provide a context that facilitates a realistic self-appraisal and helps develop self-management skills in dealing with discrimination.

Second, entering minority students must learn advocacy skills. They may learn to articulate social and political positions that can help create an equitable and fair campus environment. All of the isms — racism, sexism, and ageism — are alive and growing on college campuses. Realizing this fact may help students develop coping and self-management skills while validating their beliefs and values. These skills may help them respond proactively to injustices they may encounter in college.

Third, entering minority students must manage the campus environment in ways that promote cultural identity development. Finding a cultural niche, a place for enhancing cultural identity, promotes a greater sense of belonging which, in turn, facilitates development. This niche may be a culture room, culture-specific clubs or organizations, or it may involve getting involved in social protest activities. Entering minority students must increase their sense of belonging through redefining the environment culture specifically. Maintaining a strong ethnic identification is essential for development of a healthy minority adult (Sue, 1981; Jackson, 1976).

These tools will help entering minority students develop in all areas of their lives: academic, interpersonal, physical, values, sexual, and career development. Collectively, these tools help create an atmosphere conducive to learning, overall development, and ultimately, graduation.

Orientation Programs for Entering Minority Students

What does all this mean for planning and implementing orientation programs that meet the needs of minority students? In some instances, programs for traditional students may meet minority student needs, if those programs are done with some awareness of the unique development of minorities. In other instances, minority students may require activities that are not always applicable to traditional entering students. When developing programs and activities that meet the needs of entering minorities, orientation planners should (1) examine the philosophical assumptions of programming, (2) identify institutional characteristics, (3) assess developmental needs of entering minorities, (4) consider the selection of appropriate staff, and (5) relate programs to minority retention.

Philosophical Assumptions of Programming. Orientation programs should introduce entering minorities to the campus and should provide an assurance of belonging, an understanding of academic and social expectations, and a knowledge of campus resources (Smith and Baruch, 1981). They must promote students' connectedness to culture-specific academic, student service, and out-of-class learning activities which will link entering minorities with each other. In that sense, it is especially important for orientation programs to foster a sense of community. For entering minorities, group activities may be preferred to those done alone. Entering minorities who have a feeling of community may increase ownership to the campus and enhance their belief that they belong there.

Orientation programs should actively promote intellectual and personal development and should create an atmosphere that stimulates and motivates entering minorities to accept new challenges. This need should be met in a way that respects individual cultural values and backgrounds.

Successful orientation programs for entering minorities are those that take, as a basic premise, the idea that entering minorities have the same right to attend college as traditional students. They are equally as advantaged as traditional students, even though they hold world views and values different from traditional students. This last premise is especially important to reinforce at all levels of programming, because entering minorities may arrive on campus from other environments that may not always have perceived them as advantaged and having a right to attend school. Entering minority students must first experience the campus as one that supports and challenges them, but also one that preserves and enhances their cultural identities.

Institutional Characteristics. There are several characteristics of institutions that may influence orientation activities for entering minorities. These characteristics need to be examined carefully to develop effective orientation programs and activities for entering minorities. Certainly, variables such as campus size, racial composition of campus, financial resources, and political climate influence orientation activities for entering minorities by determining the institution's commitment to them. But other factors may affect orientation programs for entering minorities and thus need to be examined. For example, a college with limited success in admitting and matriculating minorities may place greater emphasis on how entering minorities can orient themselves to campus than one with a high retention rate. In other words, how students are retained on the campus may be an important factor for orientation programs to consider in planning activities.

Retention of entering minorities is important to orientation programs and activities and is the most cost-effective role for orientation programs for entering minorities. Boyd (1982) observed that "the key to minority student retention is not successful programs for the minority student, but basic institutional changes which make special programs unnecessary. Any program that does not contribute to that long-range goal is a bad investment of the institution's dollar" (p. 17).

Ideally, a successful orientation program for entering minorities is one that becomes obsolete, meaning there is no longer any need for a special orientation program to exist. An institution should become so responsive to its entering students' needs — students who will be brown and black in increasing numbers — that a culture-specific orientation program would become unnecessary. Thus, an institution's responsiveness is critical to the success of orientation programs and activities for entering minorities.

Another important characteristic is the amount of real or perceived discriminatory practices that occur on campus. Orientation programs for minorities must support and demonstrate ways to reduce racial prejudice and bias on the campus. For example, at one midwestern university, a large Rebel flag was flown from the window of a residence hall. For traditional entering students, this flag may not have been seen as offensive. However, for entering minority students, that flag may have portrayed an entirely different picture of the campus, one that might have said, "You don't belong here." This impression contributes to self-doubt and feelings of threat and anxiety. This university, as one might expect, has a high minority attrition rate attributable in part to mixed messages from events like the Rebel flag. Orientation activities also reflect the same mixed message.

These implicit messages must be examined carefully for racial or ethnic bias because minority retention may be affected. If systems interventions are required, then chief student affairs officers should be consulted when appropriate. Entering minorities should feel the campus welcomes them and supports their growth.

Developmental Needs of Entering Minorities. Orientation programs and activities for entering minorities must be concerned with meeting developmental needs. Several developmental factors are important: (1) expanding culture-specific skills and (2) acquiring appropriate academic, technical, and life skills. The following orientation program is illustrative of these points.

The Pilot Educational Program (PEP) of General College at the University of Minnesota (Zanoni, 1980) was designed to increase retention of American Indians, Chicanos, and blacks. The orientation program included three parallel but culturally distinct academic support programs for the three groups, beginning in the 1979–80 school year. These courses were intended to meet culturally specific social needs while teaching interdisciplinary academic skills. Courses included skill development modules, culture-specific values courses, and tutorial support seminars. Economic, social, educational, and survival information was provided in addition to advice and counseling. Instructors met and collaborated weekly to discuss mutual concerns. Results showed that the overall retention rate of PEP students increased from 59 percent in 1979–80 to 70 percent in 1980–81.

As seen from the PEP program, entering minorities learned academic skills but did so within a culture-specific learning environment which helped promote continued development of culture-specific skills. Such orientation activities appear to communicate the message, "We will respect your cultural identity while you learn," which is an essential message for entering minorities to receive.

Also, orientation programs should aid entry into culturally appropriate adult roles by placing responsibility on entering minority students to learn. This fact is especially important for those whose earlier experiences did not support appropriate role development.

Acquiring self-responsibility and self-determination skills are central to appropriate role and identity development and are important for orientation programs and activities.

Finally, it is important for entering minorities to acquire self-appraisal, self-evaluation, and self-management skills early in their college experience. These skills help students recognize their own developmental needs and contribute to successful achievement and attainment of personal goals.

Selection of Staff. Many orientation programs involve teaching faculty and student services personnel. It is important for minorities to meet faculty, who should be active in orientation activities for entering minorities. It is particularly critical that entering minorities know minority faculty personally; they serve as role models from which students may acquire culturally specific knowledge. Also, minority faculty may be especially helpful in redefining the campus to make it more culturally appropriate to students' needs. They may later become advisers or mentors to entering minorities.

Entering minorities must learn to interact with traditional students and nonminority faculty and administrators. By interacting with nonminority administrators and faculty, entering minorities will learn not to feel threatened by or anxious among them. Orientation programs and activities should encourage college administrative staff, including the college president, to attend orientation activities for entering minorities. Entering minorities may feel an increased sense of self-importance and self-confidence if they perceive administrators and faculty are concerned about their entry to college. Also, entering minority students can learn skills from administrators, such as how to manage the system and how to obtain access to those in decision-making positions. These skills are valuable life skills which are important to learn early in the college experience.

Finally, orientation programs should involve people who accurately reflect a diversity of face and gender. An equitable representation of staff creates a supportive climate in which entering minorities may develop. Seeing positive role models interacting with one another sets a healthy expectation that students, too, can interact with diverse individuals and achieve personal success in college.

Relationship to Retention. In a review of retention studies, several key factors appear to influence retention of entering minorities and are important for orientation programs and activities. These factors include a positive self-concept (Tracey and Sedlacek, 1982; DiCesare, 1970; Simmons and Maxwell-Simmons, 1978); a supportive institutional atmosphere (Turner, 1980), and financial aid (Coulson, 1981).

All these factors should be taken into account in developing orientation programs and activities. However, by no means does the obligation to orientation end here. As entering minorities come to college better prepared academically, the issues that retain them at college may change. Orientation programs cannot be stationary in their responsibility to retention. Rather, the changing values of entering minority students requires that programs and activities be state-of-the-art if they are to aid retention. One such state-of-the-art program at the University of Texas at Austin appears to create a supportive climate for entering minorities and helps their retention.

Several years ago two minority student groups, La Amistad I and UNIT, were established to provide individual and group support to entering Hispanic and black students at the University of Texas. Building on suggestions from these groups, the Welcome program began in 1978 and was designed to give entering minority students a resource by matching entering students (Welcomees) with upper class minority students (Welcomers). The Welcome program guides the Welcomee through the first few weeks on campus by answering questions about registration, classes, professors, campus organizations, and being a friend. Orientation activities are sponsored through this program every semester. The personal interaction between the Welcomer and the Welcomee, or entering student, is the successful aspect of the program. With the assistance of the Minority Student Services within the Dean of Students' Office, entering minorities meet faculty and staff at receptions, picnics, socials, and support services. Increased input with students and staff has produced the greatest personal satisfaction for entering minorities. The program has increased its activities so that, today, the Welcome program enjoys a great deal of student and faculty interaction; increased retention of minorities has been an outcome.

Orientation programs and activities for entering minorities are often integrated into other academic support programs. Orientation programs and activities have a direct relationship to retention of minorities on campus. These programs and activities help ensure a smooth transition to and entry onto the college campus for entering minorities. They motivate students to achieve and to initiate activities that preserve their cultural identities, develop a responsive campus environment, increase self-enhancement, and ultimately, help them graduate from college.

Summary

This chapter has attempted to provide insight into orienting entering minority students. It included a discussion of the social, political and historical events that influenced entering minorities' admittance to predominantly white campuses. Several characteristics of entering minority students were identified including (1) common experience of oppression, (2) sense of community spirit, (3) importance of family, (4) role of being the first to attend college, and (5) intragroup heterogeneity of ethnic groups.

The importance of education as a means of social mobility was noted. The road to achieving that goal involved two prior educational experiences, busing and the phenomenon of being the only one, which may significantly affect entering minority students. The developmental needs of entering minorities were examined, suggestions for facilitating development of entering minorities were made, and the limitations of using traditional developmental theories were outlined.

Strategies for developing or enhancing orientation programs were enumerated; these included a strong need to encourage students to retain their cultural identities while acquiring academic skills. The importance of connecting with minority peers and with minority and traditional faculty was highlighted. The role of orientation programs and activities in the retention of minorities was described. Finally, suggestions for increasing retention through orientation programs and activities were identified.

If institutions are really commited to providing equal opportunity for college success, they must not only grant access. They must develop orientation programs and activities that help minority students make a successful transition from their previous environments to the collegiate environment. Access without orientation is worse than no access at all, for it will further alienate and frustrate already oppressed young adults.

References

Astin, A. W. "Equal Access in Higher Education: Myths or Reality?" *University of California at Los Angeles Educator,* 1977, *19,* 8–17.

Baldwin, J. A. "Notes on an Africentric Theory of Black Personality." *Western Journal of Black Studies,* 1981, *5* (3), 172–179.

Boyd, W. M. "The Secret of Minority Retention." *AGB Reports,* 1982, *24* (March/April), 17–21.

Coulson, J. E. *Evaluation of the Special Services for Disadvantaged Students (SSDS) Program: 1979–80 Academic Year.* Santa Monica, Calif.: System Development, 1981.

Cross, W. E. "The Negro-to-Black Conversion Experience." *Black World,* 1971, *20,* 13–25.

DiCesare, A. *Nonintellectual Correlates of Black Student Attrition.* College Park: Maryland University Cultural Study Center, 1970.

Jackson, G. "The African Genesis of the Black Perspective in Helping." *Professional Psychology,* 1976, *7* (3), 292–308.

Nobles, W. "Extended Self: Rethinking the So-Called Negro Self-Concept." In R. L. Jones (Ed.), *Black Psychology.* (2nd ed.) New York: Harper & Row, 1980.

Porter, J. M. "Race, Socialization, and Mobility in Educational and Early Occupational Attainment." *American Sociological Review,* 1974, *39,* 303–316.

Richardson, E. H. "Cultural and Historical Perspectives in Counseling American Indians." In D. W. Sue (Ed.), *Counseling the Culturally Different: Theory and Practice.* New York: Wiley, 1981.

Richmond, M. "Strategies for Recruiting Minority Students." *College Student Journal,* 1979, *13* (Summer), 200–205.

Ruiz, R. A. "Cultural and Historical Perspectives in Counseling Hispanics." In D. W. Sue (Ed.), *Counseling the Culturally Different: Theory and Practice.* New York: Wiley, 1981.

Sedlacek, W., and Webster, D. W. *Admission and Retention of Minority Students in Large Universities.* Research Report No. 3–77. College Park: University of Maryland, 1977.

Simmons, R., and Maxwell-Simmons, C. *Principles of Success in Programs for Minority Students.* Hoboken, N.J.: Stevens Institute of Technology, 1978.

Smith, D. H., and Baruch, B. M. "Social and Academic Environments of Black Students on White Campuses." *Journal of Negro Education,* 1981, *50* (Summer), 299–306.

Sue, D. W. *Counseling the Culturally Different: Theory and Practice.* New York: Wiley, 1981.

Sue, D. W., and Sue, D. "Barriers to Effective Cross-Cultural Counseling." *Journal of Counseling Psychology,* 1977, *24.*

Thomas, G. *Black Students in Higher Education: Conditions and Experiences in the 1970s.* Westport, Conn.: Greenwood Press, 1981.

Tracey, T. J., and Sedlacek, W. E. *Noncognitive Variables in Predicting Academic Success by Race.* Paper presented at the annual meeting of the American Educational Research Association, New York: March 19–23, 1982.

Turner, R. "Factors Influencing the Retention of Minority Students in the 1980s: Opinions and Impressions." *Journal of Nonwhite Concerns in Personnel and Guidance,* 1980, *8,* 204–214.

Zanoni, C. P. "The 1979–80 General College Retention Program." *Final Report: Pilot Educational Programs.* Minneapolis: Minnesota University General College, November, 1980.

Doris J. Wright is a psychologist in the Counseling, Learning, and Career Services Program of the Counseling-Psychological Services Center at the University of Texas at Austin.

Disabled students offer a special challenge to orientation planners. These students must be mainstreamed into regular orientation programs and given special attention, particularly prior to enrollment.

Orienting Disabled Students

Brenda G. Hameister

This chapter will discuss orientation from the perspective of students with disabilities. The developmental dimensions in Chapter One will be used to identify and understand the orientation needs of disabled students. Both mainstreamed and separate strategies for orientation programming will be discussed.

Students with physical or mental disabilities are an increasingly visible and vocal minority group on today's campuses. Although disabled students have always attended college, the passage of Section 504 of the 1973 Rehabilitation Act has stimulated the enrollment of disabled students and required institutions to make necessary accommodations. Section 504 mandates equal opportunity for qualified handicapped people in the education programs and activities of all recipients of federal financial assistance, which include virtually every college and university.

Elementary and secondary schools are sending more disabled students to college. Early intervention efforts, programs for parents, and support services — such as speech and hearing therapy, physical therapy, learning support centers, and counseling — have enabled more disabled students to complete high school and look ahead to college.

There are several types of disabling conditions. These include (1) mobility impairments — students who use crutches, canes, wheel-

M. L. Upcraft (Ed.). *Orienting Students to College.* New Directions for
Student Services, no. 25. San Francisco: Jossey-Bass, March 1984.

chairs, or walk unaided but with difficulty; (2) visual impairments—students who are partially sighted or blind; (3) hearing impairments—students who are hearing impaired or deaf; (4) learning disability—students with average or above average intellectual potential who have mild to severe difficulties in reading, calculating math, listening, writing, or relating socially; and (5) speech impairments—students with articulation problems, esophageal speech, stuttering, or aphasia.

Disabled students do not represent a homogeneous population. In fact, the population is an open one; anyone may join at any time (Bowe, 1980). Unlike some other minority groups, disabled persons do not share common experiences or a common heritage which might otherwise serve to unite them (Feinblatt, 1981). Instead, disability cuts across all ages, ethnic groups, religions, and socioeconomic groups. Disabled people also have varying feelings about their disability and varying understandings of helpful academic accommodations for their specific strengths and limitations.

Perhaps a few examples will help to clarify this idea.

Bill is a legally blind student from out of state whose very high SAT scores earned him a scholarship. He used taped textbooks and a reading machine in high school and uses public transportation independently. Bill's parents are somewhat fearful of his going far away from home to attend college, but Bill is enthusiastic.

Karen is a deaf woman in her mid-thirties, married, and employed at a local industry. She is working in a technical position and needs a college degree in order to be considered for promotion. Karen communicates with manual communication—sign language—and speechreading—lipreading. She is apprehensive about taking college courses after years away from school and is unsure about which courses to take first.

Robert is a young man with quadriplegia who uses a motorized wheelchair and requires extensive personal care. He was not a strong student in high school and was not planning to attend college. However, when an accident left him disabled, he could not continue his factory job. He is entering college with uncertain career goals and serious academic deficiencies.

Although Bill, Karen, and Robert are all disabled students, they enter college with vastly different academic and interpersonal skills, needs, and expectations. A successful orientation program should provide programs and activities for disabled students that recognize their diversity.

Developmental Dimensions of Disabled Students

It would be a mistake, however, to assume that disabled students are significantly different from their able-bodied peers. As a general rule, students with disabilities are more like able-bodied students than unlike them. Karen's concern about returning to the classroom and Robert's uncertain career goals are not unusual or unique to disabled students. Basic assumptions about the developmental dimensions of entering students and their transition to college discussed in Chapter One apply to disabled students as well as to able-bodied students. A look at how the developmental dimensions identified in earlier chapters apply to disabled students follows.

Developing Intellectual and Academic Competence. Disabled students are academically qualified and capable of competing intellectually with other students. They share the usual student concerns about handling college-level academic work, but they do have some unique concerns. Will the college allow untimed tests for a dyslexic student or oral tests for a blind student? Will a sign language interpreter or an oral interpreter be available for a deaf student? Will the academic adviser be supportive of the disabled student's choice of major?

Establishing and Maintaining Interpersonal Relations. Friendships are especially important for some disabled students. Friends are needed for relaxing, learning, and sharing but also, in some cases, for providing assistance. A hearing student might be asked to assist with phone messages for her deaf roommate. Friends of a wheelchair user might help out by opening heavy doors.

Disabled entering students may be apprehensive about building new friendships that will provide necessary support. Interpersonal skills are vital in reducing uneasiness in able-bodied peers and faculty and in establishing mutually beneficial friendships.

Developing a Sex-Role Identity and a Capacity for Intimacy. It should be unnecessary to point out that disabled students are also developing sex-role identities and making decisions about sexual activity. Some students with visible disabilities find that others are uncomfortable viewing them as adults with sexual interests. At Penn State University, a discussion about disability and sexuality is one of the most popular meeting topics for the disabled student organization. Students are looking for role models and are keenly interested in meeting couples in which one or both of the partners are disabled.

Deciding on a Career and Life-Style. The career decision process is essentially the same for disabled students as for able-bodied students. Students try to formulate career objectives that maximize abilities and are consistent with interests, values, and salary needs (Sampson, 1982).

McLoughlin (1982) points out that people with physical disabilities have a substantial need for the economic benefits of a college education. Orthopedic equipment — wheelchairs, braces, and prosthetic devices; specially-equipped vehicles; structural alterations of homes; and modified household equipment all add to the ordinary expenses of living.

In addition, disabled students must consider the job tasks that are best suited to their specific abilities and disabilities. Will a student with a moderate speech impairment be hired as an elementary school teacher or a rehabilitation counselor? Will a legally blind student work quickly and accurately enough to be a competitive employee in business? Students may ask orientation or career counseling staff these questions when considering career goals.

Maintaining Personal Health and Wellness. The belief that all disabled students are ill and in need of constant medical attention is inaccurate and outdated. Although some students do require frequent medical monitoring, for example, students with some forms of cancer or severe diabetes, many others are in excellent health in spite of physical conditions that are both stable and chronic. For both groups, the challenge is to maintain a level of wellness in a new environment. Physical therapy, occupational therapy, or adaptive physical education may help to develop or strengthen new physical skills and endurance. Increased stress, decreased sleep, altered diet, and new physical demands such as long treks across campus or long study sessions challenge the personal health balance of all students. Disabled students are no exception.

Formulating an Integrated Philosophy of Life. For all students, family values, religious background, and the examples of peers are potent factors in forming personal value systems. A positive self-concept is also vital to this process; the presence of a disability can significantly affect self-concept. For newly disabled students, the disability often looms as a major part of the self-concept. After a traumatic injury, one student found that the college experience helped to "reassess my own values and stereotyped view of the disabled" and to "focus on myself as a person rather than a disability" (Pollard, 1981).

Some disabled persons enter college from a highly protective environment where they have been recognized for inabilities rather than abilities and have been included in activities with only limited expectations (Huss and Reynolds, 1980). Some students with severe mobility impairments, for example, may never have tried to dress themselves fully, to open doors, or to do personal laundry. As students leave the home environment and master some of these tasks, self-esteem increases and family relationships change.

For many disabled students, however, the disability represents a very small part of the total self-concept. Students identify themselves by characteristics such as hometown, academic major, age, or interests — not by an inability to read small print or a need for crutches.

Disabled students are developing in all of these dimensions while simultaneously learning to adapt to a new collegiate environment. If students confront physical and attitudinal barriers on campus, their developmental progress in one or more of these dimensions could be affected. For example, if a lack of curb cuts results in students traveling lengthy, circuitous routes, the time and energy available for studies, friendships, and health maintenance will be reduced. Disabled students who have concerns about their own sexuality may spend an inordinate amount of time and energy attempting to resolve this issue (Armstrong and Manley, 1981). Participation in sex eduation or counseling programs should ease concerns about sexuality and free attention for other developmental tasks.

A collegiate environment that offers physically accessible locations, accepting and encouraging attitudes, and intellectual stimulation should be the goal of orientation programs. The orientation year can introduce the disabled entering student to these opportunities.

Timing of Orientation Programs

Many disabled students ask for information about institutional services and programs well in advance of arrival day and formal orientation sessions. This information is often used in choosing which colleges to apply to and which ones to attend. Some examples follow:

A male deaf student requests information about the number of deaf students enrolled and the extent of services provided when he considers which schools to apply to. Before arrival day, he asks about locating note-takers and about installing his wake-up device on the residence hall bedstead.

In May, a female student transferring to campus in September phones to ask about wheelchair seating for fall semester sports events.

A male international student with a mobility impairment, who plans to attend a campus in the northern United States, writes several letters in June and July to ask about snow removal and modes of winter transportation.

Other examples of orientation activities are listed below, according to the usual time period in which they occur. Although not inclusive of all developmental dimensions, these types of activities occur at three general stages of orientation and can be used for planning the timing and type of programs and activities for disabled students.

Before Arrival

1. Request information about support services and modified facilities.
2. Explore institution's attitude toward students with disabilities.
3. Acquire skills and personally prescribed equipment, such as a hearing aid or spare set of crutches, necessary for new academic and physical environment.

Orientation Day

1. Attend orientation activities available to all students.
2. Attend separate orientation for disabled students, if offered.
3. Meet roommate and peer group.
4. Adjust to new housing or to new commuting pattern.
5. Adjust to new physical environment of campus.
6. Begin academic tasks: register for classes, purchase books.

Remainder of First Year

1. Seek out new information as interests change.
2. Extend social relationships.
3. Consider other housing options: new residence hall area or apartment.
4. Learn about larger physical environment both on and off campus.

Parents of traditional age disabled students are especially important in the prearrival stage. Parents often encourage their disabled sons and daughters to begin looking at colleges very early in their high school careers. A parent often makes the initial telephone or letter contact to request information about support services. Parents are active participants in campus visits, asking probing questions about admission requirements, financial aid, and the extent of services provided.

Orientation programming for disabled entering students can be divided into two main strategies. The first strategy is a mainstreamed approach that incorporates disabled students' needs into the institution's formal orientation program. The second strategy consists of information sharing and skill building directed toward the unique concerns of disabled students, both individually and in groups. Many institutions use both strategies in developing orientation programs for disabled students.

Mainstreamed Approach to Orientation

All postsecondary institutions covered by Section 504 must use mainstreamed approaches to orientation. Section 504 specifies that any separate programs, such as orientation, will be in addition to, not in place of, existing programs.

Orientation sessions should be held in wheelchair accessible locations. This is especially important for large events such as college-wide meetings or presidential receptions. For example, at Penn State University, many orientation sessions are offered simultaneously and some sessions are repeated several times. At least one session of each program is offered in a wheelchair accessible location.

It is helpful to disabled entering students to indicate which orientation sessions are accessible to persons with mobility impairments. This can be done by printing a symbol, such as the international wheelchair symbol, next to scheduled accessible events. Orientation publications should be available in large print, braille, and cassette tape for students who do not read standard print. Manual or oral interpreters should be available as needed for deaf students. Large-print handouts for sight-impaired students and written scripts of audiovisual presentations for deaf students should also be available.

Parents of traditional age students also participate in orientation sessions at many schools. Orientation presenters should understand the institution's philosophy of nondiscrimination and know where to refer parents for specific information concerning accommodations. Publications written for parents should include the location and phone number of the person or office responsible for disabled student services. Publications containing photographs of the student body should include photos of disabled students as well as students belonging to other minority groups.

Overall, making minor accommodations in existing orientation programs demonstrates an institution's concern for each student's welfare and enables students with disabilities to start out with an integrated orientation experience. A mainstreamed approach also allows able-bodied students an opportunity to increase their awareness of disabilities and accommodations (Olson, 1981).

Separate Approaches to Orientation

Individual efforts during orientation consist of everything from arranging for test accommodations in placement tests to sharing information about wheelchair accessible restaurants. Individualized sharing of information is a very important part of orientation for disabled students. Staff working with disabled students for the first time should be assured that informational, technological, and personnel resources are vast.

A good starting point for novice staff is the *Annotated Bibliography of Information Sources* published by the Association on Handicapped Student Service Programs in Post-Secondary Education (Jarrow, 1983). A second comprehensive resource is the HEATH Resource Center at One Dupont Circle, N.W., Washington, D.C. 20036, which publishes information on campus programs to integrate disabled students, technical services, and compliance with Section 504 regulations. The *New Directions* series published by Jossey-Bass contains four volumes that expand upon mainstreamed and individualized approaches to disabled student services within the context of a student development model (Redden, 1979; Sprandel and Schmidt, 1980; Wilson, 1982; Schmidt and Sprandel, 1982).

Many institutions encourage independence in disabled students, which means providing clear, accurate, and timely information about university and community resources during orientation. Topics of interest to many disabled students and their families include (1) transportation to and from campus and on campus; (2) parking on campus; (3) in-class assistance provided—such as note-takers, interpreters, laboratory assistants, and so on; (4) sources of out-of-class assistance—tutors, typists, readers, and personal care attendants; (5) financial aid sources specifically for students with disabilities; (6) adaptive physical education; (7) architectural barriers on campus; (8) housing accommodations available on campus or accessible housing off campus; and (9) resources of the disabled student services office or disabled student coordinator.

Individual orientation efforts may occur at any time during the first year. A variety of formats may be used, including individual meetings with student services staff or meetings with upper class disabled students who share similar accommodation needs. Peer contact can be very helpful for answering questions and reducing fears. Written publications such as a disabled student handbook, access map of campus, or student services newsletter should be provided in taped, braille, or raised-line forms, as appropriate. Meetings with other campus staff and faculty about their services are also useful for individual student orientation.

It is important to develop support for disabled student services among the campus staff and faculty who are meeting with disabled entering students and their families. Staff and faculty at the residence halls, campus library, and academic departments, for instance, should be knowledgeable about and interested in including disabled students fully in their programs.

Since families of disabled entering students have questions and concerns also, opportunities for communication with families should be created. At Southern Illinois University, the disabled student services office is open on arrival day for entering students, even if this occurs on a weekend. After classes have started, occasional correspondence and phone calls from parents should be expected. Parents will often alert the institution to problems that students are having but which they have not mentioned. Direct parent-university staff contact usually occurs early in the entering student's first year, before self-confidence, assertiveness, and familiarity with the institution have fully developed.

In individual contacts, the disabled student will be an important source of information about needed services. Two important cautions apply. First, don't assume that every student with a disability will want or require services or special attention. Many do not. Second, don't assume that students with the same medical diagnosis share the same functional skills. There are many degrees and types of compensatory techniques. What works well for one blind student, for example, may actually be useless for another.

Group approaches to orientation will vary with the size and type of institution, number of disabled students expected, and preference of the planning staff. Informal meetings and receptions have been held at Southern Illinois, Syracuse, and Penn State Universities at the beginning of the fall semester, when information about university services is available. Another type of informal group orientation is a picnic for entering and continuing disabled students held at the University of Wisconsin–Madison. Transportation is arranged by university staff.

An example of a formal orientation program is the four-day program for disabled students at Wright State University. Disabled students arrive on campus early for this program, which covers services available on campus and disability-related issues such as problem-solving techniques, building a relationship with a roommate, and emergency evacuation. Wright State also offers separate group orientation programs for deaf and for learning disabled students, while encouraging all disabled students to participate in the general university orientation programs.

Group orientation programs can continue throughout the year. Disabled student organizations help to orient entering students by developing social skills, leadership skills, and a positive self-concept (Baier and Putteet, 1982). Peer support groups run by disabled students are also helpful. Those offered at the University of Wisconsin–Madison are an example.

All separate, group orientation activities should not be in conflict with other important orientation sessions. Meetings or receptions should be informal and fun as well as informative. Low attendance at group activities during orientation week may actually signify success in meeting students' needs individually before arrival day.

Summary

It is difficult to remember when working with disabled students that these students are seen by others as disabled. Alert minds, fun-loving personalities, and physical abilities of all kinds abound. Individuals with disabilities are quickly seen as having attributes far more important than their physical limitations, whether it is a love of sports, a talent for photography, or a way of making people feel at ease.

The most effective way of changing attitudes and successfullly mainstreaming disabled students into existing orientation programs will be for more and more disabled students to attend orientation programs and make their needs known. As orientation staff increase their contact with disabled students, they will be more likely to remember the minor accommodations needed to ensure full access by all.

It is likely that some degree of individualized orientation will always be necessary for some disabled students. This will usually involve sharing of information about campus policies and resources to allow the student to participate fully in campus activities.

References

Armstrong, M., and Manley, S. "Sexual Counseling and Education for the Disabled College Student—A Look at Attitudes and Counseling Techniques." *The Accessible Institution of Higher Education: Opportunity, Challenge, and Response.* The proceedings of the Association on Handicapped Student Service Programs in Post-Secondary Education, Boston, July 1981.

Baier, J. L., and Putteet, T. S. "A Critical Need: Adaptive Student Development Training Programs for Disabled Students." *Journal of the National Association for Women Deans, Administrators, and Counselors,* 1982, *45* (4), 20–25.

Bowe, E. *Rehabilitating America. Toward Independence for Disabled and Elderly People.* New York: Harper & Row, 1980.

Feinblatt, A. "Political Activism Among Physically Disabled Individuals." *Archives of Physical Medicine and Rehabilitation,* 1981, *62* (8), 360–364.

Huss, J., and Reynolds, D. "Taking Charge: Assertive Behavior and Leadership Skills for Disabled College Students." *The Handicapped Student on College Campuses — Advocacy, Responsibility, and Education.* The proceedings of the Association on Handicapped Student Service Programs in Post-Secondary Education Conference, Denver, May 1980.

Jarrow, J. E. (Ed.). *Annotated Bibliography of Information Sources.* Association on Handicapped Student Service Programs in Post-Secondary Education, P. O. Box 21192, Columbus, Ohio 43221.

McLoughlin, W. P. "Helping the Physically Handicapped in Higher Education." *Journal of College Student Personnel,* 1982, *23,* 240–246.

Olson, G. S. "Handicapped Student Services: Whose Responsibility?" *Journal of the National Association of Student Personnel Administrators,* 1981, *19* (2), 45–49.

Pollard, B. "Socialization of the Disabled College Student." *The Accessible Institution of Higher Education: Opportunity, Challenge, and Response.* The proceedings of the Association on Handicapped Student Service Programs in Post-Secondary Education Conference, Boston, July 1981.

Redden, M. R. (Ed.). *Assuring Access for the Handicapped.* New Directions for Higher Education, no. 25. San Francisco: Jossey-Bass, 1979.

Sampson, D. "Career Planning and Placement: Meeting the Needs of Students with Disabilities." *Journal of the National Association for Women Deans, Administrators, and Counselors,* 1982, *45* (4), 26–30.

Schmidt, M. R., and Sprandel, H. Z. (Eds.). *Helping the Learning-Disabled Student.* New Directions for Student Services, no. 18. San Francisco: Jossey-Bass, 1982.

Sprandel, H. Z., and Schmidt, M. R. *Serving Handicapped Students.* New Directions for Student Services, no. 10. San Francisco: Jossey-Bass, 1980.

Wilson, L. (Ed.). *Helping Special Student Groups.* New Directions for College Learning Assistance, no. 7. San Francisco: Jossey-Bass, 1982.

*Brenda Hameister is coordinator of services for
disabled students in the Student Assistance Center
of Pennsylvania State University.*

*Orientation programs and activities for returning adult
students must begin at the time of admission, continue
during the first few days on campus, and progress through
the entire year.*

Orienting Returning
Adult Students

Beverly R. Greenfeig
Barbara J. Goldberg

The number of traditionally aged students on college campuses is on
the decline. The Carnegie Council on Policy Studies (1980) predicts a
23 percent decline in the traditional college-bound group of eighteen-
to-twenty-four-year-olds by 1997. Offsetting this decline is an unprece-
dented increase in the number of nontraditional students. Between
1972 and 1979, total college enrollments increased by 2.3 million; about
half of this increase was due to the enrollment of part-time students
ages twenty-five and over (*Higher Education Daily,* 1980). More than
one-third of all college students are now twenty-five or older; by 1990,
11 million students will be over thirty-five. Colleges are becoming aware
that their future may depend upon recruiting and retaining the adult or
returning student. The terms *adult student* and *returning student* are used
interchangeably in this chapter to refer to students twenty-five years of
age or older who are beginning or reentering college after a break in
their formal education. To attract and keep these students institutions
must know their specific characteristics and develop policies, programs, and services that respond to their special needs.

M. L. Upcraft (Ed.). *Orienting Students to College.* New Directions for
Student Services, no. 25. San Francisco: Jossey-Bass, March 1984.

In this chapter we will describe the characteristics and unique needs of adult students and the orientation programs and activities that meet these needs. We will also suggest ways of recruiting adult students, assisting them in their transition to college, and helping them through their first year.

Characteristics of Adult Students

In order to better understand the specific needs and strengths of adult students, some general knowledge of adult development is helpful. Those responsible for orienting and retaining adult students must understand that transition is an important theme in adult development. Adulthood is often erroneously assumed to be a time of stability and little change. It is, in fact, a time filled with transitions.

Some transitions, such as returning to school or the birth of a child, are mostly positive, while others, like death or divorce, are mostly negative. Any transition involves some degree of stress (Schlossberg, Troll, and Leibowitz, 1978); even when returning to college is a positive experience, it may still be stressful. There are time demands for those who have jobs and changes in interpersonal relations as well as other stresses.

Adults often return to college because of some transitional stage in their personal or career life. Returning students include those who (1) are newly separated or divorced and need to become more financially independent, (2) want or need a mid-life career change, (3) wish to reenter the job market — often women, and (4) have been laid off or have chosen to leave their jobs and return to college in order to upgrade skills and get a higher level job.

When added to other corresponding life transitions, returning to college may create multiple stresses for the adult student. Those who work with adults must have some knowledge of adult development and of the transitions that may occur in an adult's life. Chapter One mentions six developmental dimensions of entering students: academic competence, sexuality, personal health, career and life-style, philosophy of life, and interpersonal relations. Returning adult students have dealt with these same developmental issues during their young adult years and made certain choices at that time. As they return to college, adult students may "take stock of their dreams, their achievements, and their options" (Schlossberg, Troll, and Leibowitz, 1978, p. 17). In individual counseling with returning students we frequently encounter this stock taking in comments such as "I'm embarrassed to say that I'm forty-two years old and I don't know what I want out of the rest of my life." Returning to college gives adult students an opportunity to learn more about themselves and about their choices.

Transition Issues

As returning adults make the transition from their previous environment to the collegiate environment, several issues arise. First, there is likely to be a renewed search for identity, because many returning adults have neglected their own goals and devoted most of their energies to helping others attain their goals (Lenz and Schaevitz, 1977). These students often feel lonely and isolated, and they return to college to find themselves and to redefine their identity. This search for identity is expressed in the following poem written by Linda Tossman, a former returning adult student, as she was thinking about returning to college.

On the Threshold

I STAND ON THE THRESHOLD, PLEASE SOMEONE HELP ME!

The road back is safe and secure, a cocoon against life.
But, why was I so disquieted, depressed, and confused,
                    insecure in the security of my role?

I STAND ON THE THRESHOLD, PLEASE SOMEONE HELP ME!

The house needs so much care, won't it be terribly unkept, if I
                    place priorities outside the home?
But, why at the end of the day do I find I've used any excuse
                    to do so little?

I STAND ON THE THRESHOLD, PLEASE SOMEONE HELP ME!

My mothering role seems so all consuming; how can I take time
                    from them to find my own way?
But, why do I seem to get busy with other pursuits, using time
                    when I could be with the children?

I STAND ON THE THRESHOLD, PLEASE SOMEONE HELP ME!

My husband says he is supportive, he says he wants me to grow.
But, why is there fear in his eyes toward my changing attitudes
                    and the asserting of my needs?

I STAND ON THE THRESHOLD, PLEASE SOMEONE HELP ME!

Ahead the road is unsure, the paths many; there, I alone, must
                    reach out to the unknown.
But, why do I feel the thrill of excitement mixed with the fear!

I STAND ON THE THRESHOLD, PLEASE SOMEONE HELP ME!

I don't want to go back! I must move forward!
A voice inside calls out to me,

PLEASE HELP, FOR I STAND ON THE THRESHOLD!

Second, many returning adults are suffering from low confidence and self-esteem and are very unsure of their abilities and self-worth. Although returning adults may share these feelings with traditional entering students, the difference is that the routine of school work is not new to late adolescents. They have developed informal networks that help them gain information about assignments, instructors, and exams. Returning adults often do not have these networks. In addition, their study skills may be rusty, which can lead to questions of self-worth and ability. When we ask returning adults to list their strengths and weaknesses, their list of weaknesses is often twice as long as their strengths.

Third, many returning adults, by going back to college, are assuming an additional role in life which often creates stress. A returning adult who is already a wife, mother, and community volunteer adds unfamiliar pressures, deadlines, and tensions to an already full schedule. Orientation must help returning adults develop skills for coping with these tensions and help them realize the opportunities gained from combining college with employment and family roles.

Practical Needs

Although the needs of adult students may be similar in some ways to those of traditional, late-adolescent, entering students, they are different as well. Returning adults, especially women, are more likely than most other entering students to require childcare services in order to attend classes. Frequently, they feel academically insecure and must update rusty study skills. They may have unique financial needs, because many are studying part time and are self-supporting. They may urgently need career information and counseling, because jobs and careers may have changed since their last job or educational experience. Returning adults also need to find a peer support group with which they can share their concerns about returning to school. They need to know what services and programs are available to them.

Strengths of Adult Students

Returning students are an asset to higher education because they bring specific strengths that are unique, including strong academic abilities, unique life experiences, and strong motivation.

Academic Abilities. Adults are by and large excellent students. A survey conducted by the Educational Testing Service comparing community college students eighteen-to-twenty-one years old and twenty-two-to-twenty-nine years old with students over thirty revealed that older students are less likely to experience academic problems. Only one in six students over thirty years old reported academic difficulty, compared with one in three in the two other groups. Further, older students have more clearly defined goals than younger students, find their courses more satisfying, and spend more time studying and preparing (Educational Testing Service, 1975). In spite of these findings, many returning students are unsure of themselves in the early stages of their return to school. "I didn't think I could compete with younger students. I hadn't written a term paper since high school. I studied hard and took advantage of the special study skills programs of the Returning Students Program. I didn't just pass, I got all A's and B's."

Life Experiences. Another strength that returning students have but which they rarely recognize in themselves is previous life experiences such as volunteer and work experience, parenting, and marriage and family experience. Much of this experience can be used in their curriculum, making them assets to their classes, where they are able to provide a different perspective. "I was delighted to find that in my accounting class my instructor was interested in hearing about my past work experience in the bank."

Motivation. The returning student is highly motivated. Those who return to college usually have clear reasons for continuing their education and have translated these reasons into action. They are self-motivated, self-directed, and committed to their studies. "When I was nineteen, I went to college because my parents said to go to college. Now that I'm thirty-nine, I'm going because I want to go. I really need something that can help me personally as well as to get a job ultimately. I'm here and I'm going to make it."

Orientation Programming

Returning adults represent a diversified population: working and nonworking; married and single; parents and nonparents; self-supporting and needing financial aid; graduate and undergraduate; male and female. In developing programs and services for such a diverse population, we made the following assumptions:

1. *Multiple approaches are needed.* Because adult students are a diversified population with a wide variety of needs and interests, no one approach will suffice. Academic courses, workshops, seminars, social activities, individual counseling, and peer counseling could all be used to meet their needs.

2. *Interaction with other returning students is necessary.* A major problem of returning students is isolation from eighteen-to-twenty-two year olds. Adult students can benefit from participation in a group of other adults who have similar problems and concerns (Apps, 1982). Students are a great resource for each other and can often help solve each others' problems. The importance of students-helping-students is one reason why peer counselors might be used extensively.

3. *Information and support are key components.* The availability of information and support should be the most important element or thread in all programs to orient adult students. Through individual and group activities, in person or by phone, adult students should know about and be encouraged to take advantage of the services and programs available to them. Returning adult and prospective students should feel comfortable with and have access to the information and support services they need.

4. *Coordinated approaches are needed.* The best way to orient entering returning adults is to establish a returning adult student program, staffed by professionals and trained peers. Experience with the Returning Students program at the University of Maryland demonstrates that these students are best served when there is a highly visible, active program advocating for their concerns, and providing them with appropriate programs and services. Much of what follows in this chapter is a direct result of ten years of experience in meeting the needs of returning adults through a coordinated approach.

Recruitment Programs

If an institution really wants to meet the needs of returning adults, it should start by recruiting adult students who live and work in the counties and cities surrounding the institution. Inadequate information and anxiety about academic and personal abilities cause many adults to delay the decision to return to college. The youth-oriented image projected by many institutions is an additional deterrent. An effective recruitment program should attempt to break down these barriers, help change the community's image of the institution, and let adult students know that the institution welcomes them. By attracting more adult students, the institution may make up for the declining enrollment of traditional students.

Examples of recruitment strategies include the open house and the community outreach program, each of which can be conducted primarily by peer counselors and which can be designed to develop a positive image of the institution. Both are easy to implement, relatively inexpensive, and effective. For example, of the approximately 100 persons who attended an open house program at the University of Maryland, about 60 percent eventually enrolled in the institution.

At the University of Maryland, for example, the open house is a free all-day program that offers a unique opportunity for adults in the community to visit the campus and learn about the university. In addition to introducing university services for returning students, Returning Student counselors, peer leaders, admissions personnel, academic advisers, and financial aid advisers are available to assist participants. Instant admissions are available for individuals who have definite plans to enroll at the university.

Community outreach programs are a second way of providing information to potential adult students in the community through local volunteer groups, community organizations, religious clubs, and government agencies. At these programs, materials describing university services available to community adults can be distributed. Counselors can answer questions regarding the institution and address the concerns facing adults who choose to begin or return to college.

Preenrollment Programs

During the few months before students actually start classes, all new students, and especially returning students, may be overwhelmed with questions, fears, and concerns. Until recently, preenrollment orientation programs were geared to eighteen- to twenty-two-year-old students and did not address the needs of adult students. Adult students are more interested in childcare facilities on campus than in how to get along with a roommate. Institutions need to develop preenrollment orientation programs that meet the unique needs of adult learners and to develop topics within those programs that fit those needs.

Preenrollment orientation programs should be developed that (1) provide a supportive environment, (2) inform participants about campus life for returning students, (3) provide an opportunity to share concerns about returning to school and to interact with other returning students and resource people, and (4) offer peer leaders as role models of successful returning students. Topics might include (1) definition of a returning student; (2) profile of a returning student; (3) special strengths of returning students, such as motivation, serious commitment, life experience, and excellent grades; (4) concerns of returning students, such as day care, study skills, vocational career information, and personal issues; (5) resources on the campus for returning students, such as a Returning Students Program or individual counseling.

Also, admissions issues for adult students are quite different from those of traditional students (Mendelsohn, 1980). For this reason, specially trained admissions counselors should assist returning students with such special concerns as transfer credit evaluation, scheduling problems, credit by examination, and academic alternatives. Returning students often ask, "Will my credits from twenty-five years ago still count?" or "Do I have to take the SATs for admission?" At many institutions, returning students are directed to a special returning students admissions counselor who is aware of special admissions policies, such as not requiring SATs if the prospective student has been out of school for a number of years, and other campus services for returning students. There may be academic programs in the institution that may be particularly useful to returning students, including credit by examination, independent study, and interdisciplinary programs.

Finally, institutions may want to consider a newsletter to all returning students that welcomes them to the campus and informs them of the special services available to them. A newsletter can also provide current information about workshops, group meetings, speakers, financial aid, day care, and other relevant topics.

Support Services Throughout the Year

A number of services help orient returning students throughout their first year, including special courses, workshops, peer counseling, individual counseling, informal social gatherings, and returning adult student organizations.

Credit Courses for Returning Students. These courses can assist students in their transition to campus life and can provide continuity for students throughout their first semester or later semesters. The University of Maryland offers such a course, which emphasizes the important skills and resources needed to help students succeed in college. These skills include (1) assistance in choosing a major and academic advising; (2) career planning and vocational testing; (3) reading and study skills — how to read textbooks, how to study, and how to prepare for and score higher on exams; (4) opportunities to share common concerns; (5) campus resources; and (6) time management techniques.

Class size is limited to twelve-to-fifteen students per section in order to provide for informal discussion, active participation by all class members, and an arena for self-growth. The class is taught by one of the professional counselors in the Returning Students Program. The classroom climate can best be described as a supportive learning environment which is neither a pure counseling environment nor a highly structured classroom setting. Students develop group cohesiveness and establish a sense of community by talking about courses, instructors, and personal problems. Peer networking and long-term friendships frequently develop among participants in this course.

Grades are assigned on the basis of attendance, class participation, a personal journal, and two projects — an academic skills project and a career exploration project — which require students to search for information that might be helpful to them in setting and reaching career and academic goals. Specific class topics include goal setting, time management, academic skills, career exploration, personal exploration, registration procedures, library skills, study skills, and assertiveness training.

Workshops. Workshops for returning students and potential returning students can be an effective way of orienting students. Workshops of one to two hours can allow for presentations, discussions, and experiential exercises and are led by campus faculty, staff, and returning adult peers. The preferred group size of ten to twelve students encourages a supportive atmosphere for sharing experiences. Such workshops (1) teach and provide practice in a variety of skill areas important for success in college; (2) provide a supportive environment in which participants can share common concerns related to returning to school; and (3) provide resources through reading lists, handouts, tapes, and referrals.

Workshops can also allow participants to examine their individual goals and academic expectations without the stress of classroom competition and grading. Some adults who are thinking about returning to school can use the workshops as a transition stage to prepare for and ease into their regular university courses. Others may attend workshops to develop skills in conjunction with or in response to specific course demands. Workshop participants can also meet others who share similar interests. Workshops include such topics as time management, goal setting study skills, and examination preparation.

Peer Counselors. A very important part of a comprehensive program to orient returning adult students is the use of trained peer counselors (Carter, 1978). These experienced returning adults can serve as role models for entering returning adults and can provide them with information, counseling, programs, and advice. Students selected as peer counselors should have the time, interest, and ability to do the job and should have a record of successful studenthood, including effective interpersonal relationships and high academic achievement. They should be extensively trained, preferably through academic courses, in leadership and communication skills. They should be given supervised experience in working with returning adults and provided with ongoing training and supervision by professional staff.

A peer counseling program is an effective and economical way to supplement services for the adult learners. Because peer counselors have recently gone through reentry themselves, they have a strong commitment to helping new returning students over this hurdle. Peer counselors also increase the sense of community among returning students on the campus.

Individual Counseling, Information, and Referral Services. Adult students may also need help from a professional counselor in coping with the academic, vocational, and personal issues they face in returning to college. Entering returning adults should have accurate, up-to-date information that connects them with appropriate campus and community resources by telephone and through written correspondence, printed materials, and personal contacts.

Informal Social Activities. At various times over the last few years, the University of Maryland has offered a weekly social support and information group called "Learning Lunches." These brown-bag lunches allow returning students to have lunch with other returning students as well as to meet with various campus resource personnel. Learning Lunches provide an opportunity for an informal presentation and discussion by key campus personnel. They also encourage returning students to get together and share common concerns and experiences. Topics for these lunches include (1) financial aid opportunities for returning students; (2) career exploration; (3) acadmic opportunities; and (4) special programs for special populations; commuters, minorities, and returning students.

Returning Students Organizations. Returning students need to share campus experiences informally, discuss academic concerns, and plan social get-togethers. A returning student's organization can help by (1) compiling and distributing a directory of the active membership and providing potential membership with newsletters announcing activities; (2) reserving a regular meeting room on campus for adult students to get together weekly; (3) securing funding for academic information, sharing and study skills projects, newsletters, and social activities; and (4) working with other returning adult student organizations, such as the Veterans Club, to plan and present joint activities.

However, such organizations are often difficult to sustain. With their other commitments as homemakers, parents, employees, and students, returning adults may not have sufficient time to devote to maintaining such organizations. The reason these student groups frequently fail is because they have too little support from the institution; they can be sustained on a continuing basis only with strong professional staff support.

Institutional Involvement

In addition to the specific programs already outlined, the institution as a whole must have a commitment to orient adult students. Each institution must assess the needs and learning characteristics of its own adult student population. It must examine policies and procedures such as deferred fee payments, childcare services, weekend and evening programs, and alternate class schedules to determine if they must be adjusted to support adult students. The institution must also develop a public image attractive to adult students. For example, posters, college brochures, and other printed materials should include adult students in content and pictures. Faculty and staff must be made aware of the characteristics of returning students and their effect on the classroom and the campus. Workshops can be offered to help faculty and staff better advise, instruct, and work with adult students. Finally, institutions need to connect all agencies on campus that work with adult students. A committee of representatives from interested campus agencies, administrative officers, and adult student representatives should coordinate campus efforts on behalf of adult students, serve as their advocates, and make recommendations as needed.

College administrators must recognize the opportunity to offset declining traditionally aged student enrollment by developing programs for adult students. Developing programs and actively promoting this enrollment through university publications and general media can help to increase the university's adult population.

Some final suggestions to programmers include the following:

1. Offer a workshop that will help faculty and staff understand returning students' characteristics and problems.
2. Recognize that women are more likely than men to seek out services and express their needs.
3. Connect with the staff of other agencies and develop cooperative programs if funds are limited. At an institution that has the commitment but not the resources to develop programs for returning students, staff members of other student affairs agencies such as orientation, career center, and admissions should develop joint programs and share costs.
4. Use trained peer counselors whenever possible to expand services with little additional cost. In addition to being cost effective, peer counselors are also excellent role models for returning students.
5. Review existing resources within the institution so that ongoing workshops or programs can be modified to serve

this population. For example, if there is an orientation course, reserve one section for returning students.

6. Seek information on programs being carried out in other institutions. The University of Maryland Counseling Center's Data Bank (1980) collected information from 199 institutions throughout the United States. The responses indicated that 90 percent are offering services for Returning Students and 50 percent of those institutions have expanded these services in the the the last year.

7. Evaluate programs to determine whether they are responsive to the constantly changing needs of adult students.

8. Finally, in these times of low budgets and high demand for services, the key ingredients of successful programming are professional staff and peer counselors. They must be enthusiastic, caring, supportive and, above all, committed to adult students' success in higher education.

Summary

In this chapter we have identified the issues, needs, and strengths of adult students and have suggested recruitment, preenrollment, and ongoing programs to meet their needs. We have also stressed the importance of institutional commitment to and involvement in the orientation of adult students and the critical role of professional staff and peer counselors in developing effective programs and services for returning adults. If institutions are to maintain enrollments in an era of declining enrollments of traditionally aged entering students, they must recruit and retain returning adults through comprehensive programs and services.

References

Apps, G. *Study Skills for Adults.* New York: McGraw-Hill, 1982.

Carnegie Council on Policy Studies in Higher Education. *Three Thousand Futures: The Next Twenty Years for Higher Education.* San Francisco: Jossey-Bass, 1980.

Carter, J. (Ed.). *Second Wind: A Program for Returning Women Students.* Newton, Mass.: Education Development Center, 1978.

Educational Testing Service. *Findings.* Vol. 2. Princeton, N.J.: Educational Testing Service, 1975.

Higher Education Daily, August 17, 1980.

Lenz, E., and Schaevitz, M. H. *So You Want to Go Back to School: Facing the Realities of Reentry.* New York: McGraw-Hill, 1977.

Mendelsohn, P. *Happier by Degrees.* New York: E. P. Dutton, 1980.

Schlossberg, N. K., Troll, L. E., and Leibowitz, Z. *Perspectives on Counseling Adults: Issues and Skills.* Monterey, Calif.: Brooks/Cole, 1978.

University of Maryland Counseling Center Data Bank. College Park, Md.: University of Maryland, 1980.

Beverly R. Greenfeig and Barbara J. Goldberg are co-coordinators of the Returning Students Program of the University of Maryland Counseling Center.

Transfer students must begin orientation while enrolled at their previous institution and continue it at their current institution since they will be dealing with many unique issues that are typically not included in traditional orientation programs.

Orienting Transfer Students

Charlene H. Harrison
Kenneth Varcoe

Students who enroll at one institution and change to another have become commonplace in American higher education. Recent estimates suggest that over 40 percent of students transfer at some time in their undergraduate careers (National Center for Education Statistics, 1977). These transfer students are faced with a combination of difficulties and obstacles that can be overwhelming. Moore (1981) writes that "we must ask ourselves if we have not structured the situation for transfers in which positive learning activities are just about impossible to carry out without some trauma. The result is that students receive a strong negative message about themselves and about learning" (p. 26).

This chapter will consider the needs of students who transfer and will describe approaches to orienting them, analyze the results of a recent transfer student orientation survey, and suggest a model for transfer orientation programs.

Transfer Students: Who Are They?

Transfer students are defined as those who intend to change institutions or locations or those who change locations for unanticipated

M. L. Upcraft (Ed.). *Orienting Students to College.* New Directions for
Student Services, no. 25. San Francisco: Jossey-Bass, March 1984.

reasons. Students with baccalaureate aspirations who enroll in two-year colleges or two-year branches of universities usually intend to transfer. Students enrolling in four-year institutions usually expect to complete their program without a transfer.

Students may transfer from one two-year institution to another, from a two-year to a four-year institution, from one four-year institution to another, and from a four-year to a two-year institution — frequently called a reverse transfer. Normally, the only planned transfers are from two-year to four-year institutions. Unanticipated transfers often occur because students are unhappy with the institution or because personal circumstances have changed. Students may have academic difficulties, become dissatisfied with the academic program, perceive they don't fit the institution, develop financial difficulties, choose a different career or life-style, undergo a personal crisis, or find that they must relocate because of family or employment considerations.

Transfer Students: Are They Really Different?

In many ways, transfer students have the same needs as other entering students. They, too, want to make a smooth, efficient transition to the new institution. However, transfer students differ from other entering students in many ways. Kintzer (1973) referred to transfers as educational middlemen, saying they have not been the preferred student in higher education. One thing is clear, however. They pervade higher education in unrecognized proportions, and thus, their uniquenesses should be described and analyzed.

There is considerable evidence that transfers differ from other entering students in the following ways:

1. Two-year college transfers have lower test scores and high school averages than native four-year students (Cross, 1968; Sandeen and Goodale, 1976; Chalick, 1977).

2. The grades of most two-year transfers decline during the first term after transfer and then improve in successive terms (Knoell and Medsker, 1965; Abadzi, 1980; Richardson and Doucette, 1982), but when initial achievement or admission scores are controlled, GPAs of transfers and native students are comparable (Chalick, 1977; Harrison and Zervanos, 1983).

3. Transfers have a lower retention rate than first-time entering students (Avakian, MacKinney, and Allen, 1982; Newlon and Gaither, 1980).

4. Transfers change majors more frequently than natives (Harrison and Zervanos, 1983).

5. Transfers take longer to earn their baccalaureate degrees (Harrison and Zervanos, 1983; Cohen and Brawer, 1981–1982).

6. Transfers are less likely to aspire to education beyond the baccalaureate degree than native four-year students (Cross, 1978; Harrison and Zervanos, 1983).

7. Parents of transfers are less educated and have less family income than natives (Astin and others, 1967; Knoell and Medsker, 1965; National Center for Education Statistics, 1977).

8. Transfers are more likely to work than natives (Knoell and Medsker, 1965).

9. Transfers are less likely than natives to receive scholarships, fellowships, or grants (National Center for Education Statistics, 1977).

10. Contrary to earlier work by Knoell and Medsker (1965), transfers are interested in out-of-class activities (Worley and Conrad, 1973).

11. Expectation incongruency is a factor in four-year to four-year transfers (National Center for Education Statistics, 1977).

It would be a mistake, however, to assume that all transfers are the same. In fact, they are a very heterogeneous population representing a wide spectrum of ages, races, and backgrounds. Additionally, there are some differences between students who transfer from two-year institutions and those who transfer from one four-year institution to another. For example, upper division grades of two-year college transfers are lower than those of four-year college transfers. (Kissler, Lara, and Cardinal, 1981). Whites have a greater two-year to four-year transfer rate than blacks, and blacks have a greater rate than Hispanics (National Center for Education Statistics, 1977). Finally, four-year college transfers are more interested in living in residence halls and participating in academically or personally directed activities than junior college transfers (Worley and Conrad, 1973).

Transfer Students: Their Dilemmas

Since transfers are clearly different in many respects from other entering students, it might seem that these differences would be taken into account by the institutions they enter. Frequently, this is not the case. Transfers can experience problems even before they enroll. They are sometimes unable to take required courses at their previous institution; many times financial aid and housing application deadlines occur before transfers are admitted. Transcript evaluations are delayed, or problems with evaluating credits arise, such as accepting credit by examination, credit for nontraditional courses, and credit for courses in which pass-fail grades are earned (Remley and Stripling, 1983). Transfers are often ignored by the institution and not provided with the necessary information required to make a successful transfer. Sandeen and Goodale (1972) report that only four in ten institutions develop separate orientation programs. Many times, transfers are grouped with other entering students on the incorrect assumption that the needs of both groups are served by a common program (Sandeen and Goodale, 1972). Further, many transfer orientation programs assume that transfers are a homogeneous population having the same needs and needing the same orientation (Worley and Conrad, 1973).

What Should Be Done?

Both Moore (1981) and Worley and Conrad (1973) recommend orientation programs for transfers; most programs designed for typical first-time entering students do not work for transfers. Sandeen and Goodale (1976) also suggest that transfer interests should shape the content of orientation programs. Their research determined that transfers are most interested in course selection, credit evaluation, living arrangements, and financial matters. The 1977 National Center for Education Statistics report urged better communication between sending and receiving institutions and better counseling for transfers.

Sandeen and Goodale (1976) recommended that the following factors be considered in designing transfer orientation programs:

1. Student interests be addressed, including course selection, credit evaluation, living arrangements, and financial matters.
2. Transfer programs be offered throughout the year consistent with transfer students' enrollment patterns, in other words, during both fall and off-term transfer.
3. Sessions be offered for prospective transfers the term prior to the planned enrollment period.
4. Attention be given to transfers' social adjustment and their involvement in the life of the institution.
5. Previous transfer students be involved as orientation leaders-planners in the development of these programs.
6. The attitudes held by faculty and administrators about trans-

fers be examined. Accurate data about transfer students' academic performance, ability, and concerns may provide the basis for increased faculty and administration awareness of and support for transfers.

7. A strong institutional commitment be made to transfers, including the establishment of an institution-wide orientation committee.

Sandeen and Goodale (1976) concluded that attitudes must be changed at institutions that act "as if they do not have transfers and give them little or no recognition. An effective orientation program for transfer students must take into account these human factors as well as the more obvious academic and student service needs of the student" (p. 79).

Transfer Orientation: What Currently Exists?

In May of 1983, the authors surveyed 425 four-year institutions with undergraduate enrollments of at least 3,000. A total of 174 (40.9 percent) institutions responded to the survey, which asked participating institutions to describe their orientation programs and activities for transfers. The results of this survey (Varcoe and Harrison, 1983) suggest the following generalizations:

1. Many institutions with sizable entering student populations of transfer students do not have specialized student-need based orientation programs. One hundred and nineteen (68.4 percent) of those surveyed have special programs for transfers.

2. Although some specialized programs for transfers are provided, the most common approach to orientation involves including transfers with first-time entering students for most orientation activities.

3. The typical approach to transfer orientation emphasizes transcript evaluation and academic information, advisement, and registration.

4. Several specialized transfer orientation approaches exist which could be modified by other institutions interested in developing or improving transfer orientation programs.

5. Many of the most promising orientation programs include activities and sessions during the summer or a few months prior to the beginning of classes. Seventy-four (62.2 percent) of those with transfer programs have summer sessions.

6. Ongoing — during the semester — orientation program efforts

are an area for further development; only 16 percent of the respondents indicated the existence of these opportunities.

7. Student development in the six dimensions described in Chapter One does not seem to be incorporated into the orientation programs. Academic and intellectual development and interpersonal relations are cited most frequently as program goals. The other four dimensions are cited only occasionally as being the goals of orientation.

On the basis of these findings, it appears that orientation programs for transfer students vary greatly, depending upon institutional size, the number of transfers, institutional procedures for registration and academic advisement, and the nature of the transfer population. If many students attend a two-year institution in the state or region and transfer into an articulated program, as contrasted with students transferring without coordination from a variety of institutions and locations, the orientation efforts of the receiving institution can focus specifically on the population from area institutions.

The survey results clearly demonstrate that the major emphasis in orientation programs for transfers is academic: evaluation of transfer credit, academic advisement, and registration. Many responding institutions conduct one- to two-day programs during the summer, for fall admits, that emphasize these academic concerns. Others provide abbreviated sessions immediately prior to the beginning of classes.

However, other transfer student needs such as personal adjustment and information about the institution are met through printed materials, optional transfer sessions, or optional participation in the general orientation activities. A smaller number of institutions offer comprehensive transfer orientation programs that include academic components as well as student development, general information, and personal adjustment components. Others incorporate specific sessions for transfers within a week-long comprehensive orientation program. Many institutions do not develop specialized approaches to meet the needs of transfer students. In some cases the transfer population is too small to justify a special program.

The survey results clearly demonstrate that relatively few institutions have comprehensive transfer orientation programs. Although over two-thirds of the sample have some transfer orientation components, only about 20 percent of the sample have programs that address the range of transfer student needs.

Transfer Orientation: A Model

Transfer orientation should begin with four-year institutions developing articulation programs with two-year institutions that encourage transfer students to continue their education at the next level. Next, students should obtain appropriate information and apply to the four-year institution. After admission has been offered, the four-year institution should provide general information, transcript evaluation, academic advisement, and registration information. Financial and living arrangements must also be made. Unless these basic needs are met, the transition from one institution to another will be very troublesome. Printed information and a summer orientation session can help transfers meet these needs. Transfer students must next adjust to a different physical and interpersonal environment and meet their various developmental needs. Although these concerns may be addressed in part through the institutional literature and summer sessions, they are best addressed prior to the start of classes and into the semester.

More specifically, transfer student orientation programs and activities must address (1) academic articulation, (2) academic transition, (3) living or transportation arrangements, (4) financial considerations, (5) environmental adjustment, and (6) developmental needs. These components will be examined more specifically in the following section.

Academic Articulation. Two-year institutions that have significant transfer populations should develop articulation procedures with four-year institutions. These transfer placement and advisement programs can assist students in making a smooth academic and personal transition to the four-year institution. Similarly, four-year institutions should establish academic articulation programs with the institutions that supply transfer students. Programs explaining the transfer process and transcript evaluation should be developed cooperatively where feasible.

The University of Kansas offers a one-day program for community college students in the spring that provides general information, orientation, and preregistration for the fall semester, followed by one-day sessions in the summer. Community college personnel are informed of these sessions and encouraged to assist students in meeting the admission deadlines and requirements. While the spring program has an academic emphasis, it includes other information students may find helpful to their transition.

Academic Transition. Transfers should have timely evaluation of credits by the receiving institution. A program should be offered at least a few weeks before the enrollment period — preferably late spring or early summer for fall enrollment — which includes a transcript evaluation review, academic advisement, and preregistration. This program should also include general academic information, placement testing options, opportunities for credit evaluation reviews, and options for credit by examination or life experience.

A review of current practice suggests that academic transition needs are best met by one- or two-day program offered at least one month prior to enrollment. Transfers must have been accepted for admission and must have submitted transcripts for evaluation prior to these programs. Students bring updated transcripts; after an initial general information session concerning transfer of credit and academic requirements, students are assigned academic advisers for program planning and preregistration.

Many institutions require placement tests for transfer students; this is usually done at summer orientation programs. Since some institutions provide advance placement in courses on the basis of these exams, testing opportunities early in the summer provide students with results prior to the beginning of classes.

Living or Transportation Arrangements. Either as a part of the orientation program or in conjunction with the admissions process, students must make living arrangements at the new institution. Arrangements for on-campus housing should be made as early as possible prior to enrollment; at many institutions, transfers may have a lower priority for on-campus housing than other students. If transfers intend to live off campus, they should be provided with housing lists and referrals as well as help in finding roommates. Because a large percentage of transfers, particularly those from community colleges, may live away from their parent's home for the first time, assistance with the housing arrangements can contribute greatly to a smooth transition. When the transfer student commutes from home, transportation must be arranged.

Financial Considerations. When compared to other entering students, transfers may have significant financial problems. Frequently, student financial aid priorities favor continuing students and first-time entering students. Opportunities to resolve financial aid difficulties should be provided as early as possible in the transfer admissions cycle. Transfer students may have greater financial need than other entering students; procedural delays in awarding aid may create hardships. Transfers may also need part-time employment more than other entering students and should be helped in finding such employment through the use of part-time employment referrals or listings. They frequently have more expenses and could benefit from personal financial budgeting and planning information. Short-term emergency loan funds also should be available.

Environmental Adjustment. Transfer students need to become familiar with the campus and location of facilities. Strategies for meeting this need include campus tours, information in handbooks and other college publications, and distribution of campus maps. Other students can be helpful in teaching transfers about campus facilities.

Transfers also have to adjust to a new campus climate. Frequently, transfers have fears about larger class sizes, less personal contact with faculty, and more impersonal teaching and grading. Transfers may also have difficulties with participation in extracurricular activities; registration and scheduling; and may lack familiarity with new terminology, procedures and regulations, all of which make them feel like second-class citizens.

To help students learn about physical facilities and the new campus climate, campuses should review current approaches, including both formal programs and access to the informal peer network. The University of Texas at Austin orientation literature compares transfer adjustment to an American traveling to Great Britain — "The language is similar, but not quite the same; the rules for driving are completely different; and yet travel can be such an exciting learning experience."

Small groups of transfers led by peer student leaders or students who have transferred can be a very effective way of helping transfers make a successful transition: These orientation leaders, if carefully selected and properly trained, can be a reliable information source. They can also provide student-to-student insights about the campus climate and student life. Former transfer students can be good role models for new students and can allay student fears by demonstrating their own success. Small groups of transfers led by peer leaders can also provide a much needed support group and help transfers develop their own network of social contacts.

Developmental Issues. Orientation to a new institution should include attention to the developmental dimensions identified in Chapter One, including interpersonal relations; sexuality and sex-role identity; academic and intellectual development; personal health and wellness; philosophy of life, values, and spirituality; and career and life-styles. These issues should be addressed in a comprehensive orientation program, but the timing and nature of the presentations are critical. The priority needs which transfers have — academic transition, finances, and living arrangements — must be met before they will be receptive to developmental programming. However, the orientation program should deal with interpersonal relations, particularly personal adjustment, social needs, and making friends. The peer group approach discussed above is effective in assisting transfers develop a sense of belonging and well-being.

Developmental programs may be most appropriate during new-student weeks and ongoing orientation efforts. Based on the results of the survey of orientation practices discussed earlier, it appears that many institutions do not have developmental programs as part of their orientation efforts.

Other Aspects of Transfer Orientation

The previous six components provide a basis for organizing an effective, student need-based transition orientation program. However, there are four other issues that must be considered, including (1) the timing and format of the orientation process, (2) participation of family members, (3) meeting the needs of special transfer groups, and (4) appropriate support services.

Timing and Format of the Orientation Process. Transfer students frequently have a false sense of security — they have been new students before and believe they will have few problems making the transition to another institution. Except for academic needs, transfers are often less concerned with transition needs. This overconfidence, although useful, may keep them from attending the various programs important to their successful transition. Recognizing their experience and competence while encouraging their participation in orientation is difficult, yet critical to their success. Transfer students are reluctant to attend an orientation program that is geared to first-time entering students. They are more likely to attend specially designed programs conducted by experienced transfer students.

The concept of learning readiness can be applied to the scheduling and timing of the various orientation programs. Consequently, the orientation process can be divided into three phases: preenrollment programs, orientation week programs, and ongoing programs.

Preenrollment Programs: Ideally, the orientation process begins with information provided by the college in response to an admissions application. Appropriate descriptive information about procedures involved in the admission process as well as academic information about programs of study, requirements, deadlines, transfer of credit, registration, and so on, should be provided. Transfers also need general information about housing, student aid, other student services, and student life at the campus.

Transfer credit evaluation, academic advisement, preregistration activities, housing, and student financial aid procedures should also be initiated as early as possible. The earlier these processes take place, the more likely the student is to feel comfortable with the transition.

The publications developed by the institution for transfers are one of the primary strategies available for acquainting students with the institution. Typically, these publications include information about the summer and fall orientation sessions and other pertinent information such as transfer of credits, advisement, and registration. General information about housing, student aid, other student services, and student life should be included.

In addition to written materials, on-campus sessions in the spring or summer are recommended. If these sessions are not scheduled until a few days before the term begins, students may be unable to have credit evaluations reviewed or changed. They also may have a low priority in the registration process and a lower priority for housing and student aid.

Orientation Week Programs: The few days prior to the beginning of classes at most colleges and universities are reserved for New Student Week. These programs, which range from one to several days, typically include academic and class registration activities; campus tours; presidential and deans' welcome sessions; information sessions about student and academic support services, institutional procedures, and regulations; and social activities.

Transfer students are frequently invited to these general orientation activities intended for all entering students. Although many institutions do not distinguish between transfers and first-time entering students, many institutions offer some specialized sessions for transfers. Some institutions have developed significant parallel programs designed to meet the different needs of transfers.

Ongoing Orientation Programs: Ongoing orientation opportunities such as workshops, seminars, credit courses, and so on, exist at very few institutions. However, ongoing efforts are very important to the successful transition of transfers. Developmental issues in particular can be addressed more effectively in ongoing programs.

Family Member Programs. Some institutions offer programs for parents, spouses, and guests of transfer students. The University of California at Santa Barbara summer session encourages "the people who are close to you" to visit the campus during the day-and-a-half summer transfer orientation program. Their concurrent family program includes discussions with student service administrators, advisers, professors, and students; tours; and demonstrations of educational facilities.

Parents and spouses can provide important support for transfers; family programs provide information and advice that can strengthen this support. A great opportunity to help transfers is missed if family programs are not conducted.

Special Groups. A number of institutions recognize the plurality of their student population and schedule special sessions for minorities, women, older students, disabled students, and other identified special groups. The value of these opportunities should not be underestimated in the process of transition and adjustment.

Support Services. The University of California at Berkeley has developed the Transfer Student Institute, which is designed to assist educational opportunity and affirmative action transfer students in making the transition to Berkeley. The institute presents an intensive eight-week program of courses and seminars intended to give entering transfers strong, supportive assistance to achieve academic success. Each transfer receives academic advising, extensive counseling, and tutorial support while enrolled in the credit-bearing courses.

Summary

Transfer students constitute a large percentage of entering students at many institutions of higher education. Orientation programs based on student needs will help these students make a smooth transition. Transfer orientation programs should include academic articulation; academic aspects such as transcript evaluation, academic advisement, and registration; living or transportation arrangements; financial concerns; environmental adjustment; and developmental issues including personal and social concerns. The orientation process should start during the student's admission to the institution or shortly thereafter; continue with publications and written information; include a timely — at least a month prior to enrollment — academic advisement and preregistration session; an orientation week or days immediately prior to the semester; and ongoing orientation activities. Treating transfers as a homogeneous group of students, or in the same manner as first-time entering students, is not recommended. Retention of transfers can be improved through specialized orientation programs designed to meet the diverse needs of these students in transition.

References

Abadzi, H. "The Use of Multivariate Statistical Procedures in International Student Admissions." *Journal of College Student Personnel,* 1980, *21* (May), 195–201.

Astin, A. W., Panos, R. J., and Breager, J. A. "National Norms for Entering College Freshmen, Fall 1966." Washington, D.C.: American Council on Education, 1967.

Avakian, A. N., MacKinney, A. C., and Allen, G. R. "Race and Sex Differences in Student Retention at an Urban University." *College and University,* 1982, *52* (Winter), 160–165.

Chalick, C. "A Study to Determine the Perceived Needs of Community College Transfer Students at West Chester State College." Unpublished doctoral dissertation, Nova University, 1977.

Cohen, A. M., and Brawer, F. B. "Transfer and Attrition — Points of View. The Persistent Issues." *Community and Junior College Journal,* 1981–1982, *52,* 17.

Cross, K. P. *The Junior College Student: A Research Description.* Princeton, N.J.: Educational Services, 1968.

Harrison, C. H., and Zervanos, S. M. "Academic and Social Adjustments for Commonwealth Campus Students Associated with Their Change of Assignment." A study by the ad hoc committee on the transfer student, Pennsylvania State University, July 1983.

Kintzer, F. C. *Middleman in Higher Education.* San Francisco: Jossey-Bass, 1973.

Kissler, G. R., Lara, J. F., and Cardinal, J. L. "Factors Contributing to the Academic Difficulties by Students Who Transfer from Community Colleges to Four-Year Institutions." Paper read at American Educational Research Association, Los Angeles, April 1981.

Knoell, D. M., and Medsker, L. L. *From Junior to Senior College: A National Study of the Transfer Student.* Washington, D.C.: American Council on Education, 1965.

Moore, K. M. "The Transfer Syndrome: A Pathology with Suggested Treatment." *NASPA Journal,* 1981, *18* (Spring), 22–28.

National Center for Education Statistics. *Transfer Students in Institutions of Higher Education.* Washington, D.C.: National Center for Education Statistics, 1977.

Newlon, L. L., and Gaither, G. H. "Factors Contributing to Attrituion: An Analysis of Program Impact on Persistence Patterns." *College and University,* 1980, *55* (Spring), 237–251.

Remley, T. P., Jr., and Stripling, R. O. "Perceptions of Transfer Problems Experienced by Community College Graduates." *Journal of College Student Personnel,* 1983, *24* (1), 43–50.

Richardson, R. C., Jr., and Doucette, D. S. "The Transfer Function: Alive and Well in Arizona." *Community and Junior College Journal,* 1982, *52* (May), 10–13.

Sandeen, A., and Goodale, T. "Student Personnel Programs and the Transfer Student." *NASPA Journal,* 1972, *9* (3), 179–200.

Sandeen, A., and Goodale, T. *The Transfer Student: An Action Agenda for Higher Education.* Gainesville: Institute of Higher Education, University of Florida, 1976.

Varcoe, I. E., and Harrison, C. H. *Programs That Work in Transfer Orientation.* University Park, Pa.: Pennsylvania State University, 1983.

Worley, B., and Conrad, R. "Orientation and Activities for Transfer Students: Are Freshman Models Appropriate?" *NASPA Journal,* 1973, *10* (4), 333–338.

Charlene H. Harrison is assistant director of residential life programs at Pennsylvania State University.

Kenneth Varcoe is assistant vice-president for Student Services and the Commonwealth Education System, Pennsylvania State University.

Several orientation myths are analyzed in light of the recent evidence and information presented in this sourcebook.

Orientation Programs: Myths and Realities

M. Lee Upcraft

Throughout this sourcebook, we have attempted to establish several important points about the orientation of entering students. One of the reasons for writing about orienting students to college is that, in general, colleges and universities do not really understand the importance of orientation and the useful role it can play in the mission of an institution. Not only are most institutions limited in their understanding, they frequently believe things about orientation that extensive research and experience show are not true.

Perhaps, therefore, the best way to summarize this sourcebook is to review several frequently held myths about orienting students to college and to examine those myths in the light of the evidence presented here.

1. *Myth:* Orientation programs don't really make a difference other than making entering students feel more comfortable in their new environment.

   Reality: There is evidence that participation in orientation activities can result in better academic achievement and higher retention than nonparticipation.

2. *Myth:* Orientation programs are one-shot activities at the beginning of the first semester of enrollment.

M. L. Upcraft (Ed.). *Orienting Students to College.* New Directions for
Student Services, no. 25. San Francisco: Jossey-Bass, March 1984.

Reality: Most comprehensive orientation programs begin with preenrollment programs, continue through the first few days of enrollment, and go on throughout the first year.

3. *Myth:* Orientation programs are fun and games.

Reality: Orientation programs frequently encompass such important activities as registration and academic advising and programs of academic and intellectual substance, including academic courses, workshops, and seminars.

4. *Myth:* Orientation is only for entering students.

Reality: Orientation must include not only entering students but their parents, spouses, and families as well. Orientation should also include campus faculty and staff as a way of orienting them to the entering student population.

5. *Myth:* All entering students are late adolescents fresh out of high school.

Reality: A substantial number of entering students are *not* "freshmen" in the traditional sense, and include returning adult and transfer students.

6. *Myth:* All entering students live away from home in residence halls and are therefore easily accessible to orientation.

Reality: Most entering students do not live in residence halls but at home or in off-campus apartments and are sometimes difficult to attract to orientation programs and services.

7. *Myth:* Older entering students don't need orientation. They are mature adults who can make their way in college without any orientation efforts.

Reality: Returning adult students are as confused and uncertain as traditional entering students and need orientation to help them with their unique needs.

8. *Myth:* Transfer students don't need orientation, because they have already been enrolled at another institution.

Reality: Transfer students have special problems in getting from one institution to another and are much like other entering students in that they are in a new, unknown situation.

9. *Myth:* Disabled students are significantly different than their able-bodied peers; therefore, orientation efforts should be significantly different.

Reality: Disabled students are more like able-bodied students than unlike them. They should be encouraged to participate fully in orientation activities for all entering students as well as in any special programs for the disabled.

10. *Myth:* Minority students should have significantly different orientation programs.

Reality: Minority students have unique needs that should be met not only through special programs but through orientation actaivities for all entering students that are sensitive to the unique cultural backgrounds and prior educational experiences of entering minority students.

In summary, we reiterate the major rationale for orientation programs: As higher education faces declining enrollments, institutions must not only step up recruiting efforts but retention efforts as well. There is increasing evidence, reviewed in this sourcebook, that when entering students participate in orientation programs, they increase their chances of academic success. Thus, institutions must develop comprehensive programs that meet the needs of all students.

M. Lee Upcraft is director of Counseling and Health Services of Pennsylvania State University and a member of the graduate faculty.

Index